Supporting the Young Childrei

Language and communication skills are a key foundation of child development. This accessible and engaging resource enables early years educators to support the wellbeing and development of children whose first language is not English.

Positioning language as a community entity, the book explores critical approaches to language development and, importantly, their practical application to planning, provision, professional development, and wellbeing. It provides context and evidence-based strategies to develop strong, child-centred practice in real-world settings, and offers an overview of how educators can work with families to ensure a consistent approach to early language development at home.

The book:

- Supports the wellbeing of children for whom everyday communication in an English setting may be confusing and difficult
- Provides strategies and techniques that recognise the unique wellbeing needs of children with EAL and can be implemented immediately throughout the EYFS curriculum and beyond
- Focuses on engaging the whole community with a holistic approach to early language development and wellbeing

Drawing from first-hand experience and with practical examples and ideas woven throughout, this is an essential resource for all early years educators working with young children with EAL.

Liam A. Murphy is a British-born early years educator who has spent his career exploring Asia, specifically Japan, Mainland China, and Hong Kong, where he has introduced international early years standards and practices across multiple schools and educational institutions.

Liam's passion is in language development, specifically second, third, or even fourth languages, and the development of the young brain as it acquires communication skills across vastly different communication methods.

Liam hopes to introduce more practitioners to life in the international early years system, and hopes this book helps those who are on their own adventure into multilingualism!

Little Minds Matter: Promoting Social and Emotional Wellbeing in the Early Years

Series Advisor: Sonia Mainstone-Cotton

The *Little Minds Matter* series promotes best practice for integrating social and emotional health and wellbeing into the early years setting. It introduces practitioners to a wealth of activities and resources to support them in each key area: from providing access to ideas for unstructured, imaginative outdoor play; activities to create a sense of belonging and form positive identities; and, importantly, strategies to encourage early years professionals to create a workplace that positively contributes to their own wellbeing, as well as the quality of their provision. The *Little Minds Matter* series ensures that practitioners have the tools they need to support every child.

Outdoor Play for Healthy Little Minds
Practical Ideas to Promote Children's Wellbeing in the Early Years
Sarah Watkins

Supporting the Wellbeing of Children with SEND
Essential Ideas for Early Years Educators
Kerry Payne

Supporting Behaviour and Emotions in the Early Years
Strategies and Ideas for Early Years Educators
Tamsin Grimmer

A Guide to Mental Health for Early Years Educators
Putting Wellbeing at the Heart of Your Philosophy and Practice
Kate Moxley

Supporting the Wellbeing of Children with EAL
Essential Ideas for Practice and Reflection
Liam Murphy

Building Positive Relationships in the Early Years
Conversations to Empower Children, Professionals, Families and Communities
Sonia Mainstone-Cotton and Jamel Carly Campbell

Supporting the Wellbeing of Young Children with EAL

Essential Ideas for Practice and Reflection

Liam A. Murphy

Routledge
Taylor & Francis Group

LONDON AND NEW YORK

Cover image: Mihrumah is four years old and loves creative exploration. Her school uses real life experiences to aid language development and this art is based on the 'outside' and on rainbows, one of Mihrumah's favourite things to draw.

First published 2023
by Routledge
4 Park Square, Milton Park, Abingdon, Oxon OX14 4RN

and by Routledge
605 Third Avenue, New York, NY 10158

Routledge is an imprint of the Taylor & Francis Group, an informa business

© 2023 Liam A. Murphy

British Library Cataloguing-in-Publication Data
A catalogue record for this book is available from the British Library

Library of Congress Cataloging-in-Publication Data
A catalog record has been requested for this book

ISBN: 978-1-032-04013-4 (hbk)
ISBN: 978-1-032-04011-0 (pbk)
ISBN: 978-1-003-19021-9 (ebk)

DOI: 10.4324/9781003190219

Typeset in Optima
by Deanta Global Publishing Services, Chennai, India

Contents

Foreword

This latest book in the Little Minds Matter series explores how we can support the wellbeing needs of children with English as an additional language. I am thrilled to have this book as part of our series; I found the book fascinating and so helpful. Liam is an experienced early years practitioner who has worked in several countries and currently lives and works in Hong Kong. Throughout the book, he shares his wealth of knowledge and practice working with children with EAL.

The book starts with a helpful introduction to language theory, linking to pioneer theorists and offering us a good starting point to think about what we know already and our gaps around our knowledge of language acquisition. Throughout the book, Liam weaves together theory and practice, with many opportunities to stop and reflect on our approach. This book gently encourages us to reflect on our thoughts and presumptions around children with EAL and our current practice and to question how and why we work in the way we do.

Underpinning all of this book is the vital subject of supporting children's wellbeing and recognising how children with EAL can have their wellbeing needs overlooked or unmet. Liam offers many practical ideas, tips and suggestions throughout the book to ensure we consider the unique wellbeing needs of children with EAL and how we can meet these.

This book is an essential read for every early years practitioner working with children with EAL; I am confident this will become a book for early years course reading lists. I think this is an exciting and essential addition to our professional understanding and development.

Sonia Mainstone-Cotton
Series Advisor
November 2021

An Introduction from the Author

'I see no absolute necessity why any language would be perpetually changing.'

(Jonathan Swift, Proposal for Correcting, Improving, and Ascertaining the English Tongue, *1712)*

Hello reader, and welcome to *Supporting the Wellbeing of Children with EAL*.

In this book we will be thinking about languages, specifically English as an Additional Language, and how EAL affects the social, emotional, and educational wellbeing of a child. With that topic in mind, ask yourself: what is language?

To me, language is about community, and this is the first idea I want us to become familiar with as we read this book; ***think community!***

Languages are community entities that help us to communicate our needs and wants to those around us. Language development, therefore, should also be a community entity, whether it be a first language, second language, or even a third language.

Spoken, written, listened to, and read languages are uniquely human means of communication (Hayes, 2016) and, as we know, children learn languages through play, through frequent interaction with competent users of a target language (Ferjan-Ramirez, 2017) and, this leads me into my second and third critical thoughts before we read on, arguably two of my more common sayings: ***consistency is key!*** and ***have fun!***

Language development, along with early development, requires a consistent approach from teachers, practitioners, and parents and should be

DOI: 10.4324/9781003190219-1

approached with the same vigour and enjoyment that one would approach any developing aspect of early life.

My career path has seen me travel throughout the UK, Hong Kong, Japan, and Mainland China to work with fellow educators, parents, and institutions so that they might better understand developmentally appropriate practice, specifically as it relates to language development. For educators, I hope they can better understand and infuse language development theories into their practical teaching, and for parents, I hope they can come to better understand not only how language development works, but that language, and indeed education, is a lifelong process with no real linear time frame.

This is what we will explore together in this book, a guideline with advice and tips that will apply to the real setting, simple resources to understand theory, and advice on how to infuse these into teaching practices. Further to the language aspect, there will be recommendations on early childhood education in general, helping teachers to develop strong child-centric practices and, more than anything, this book will aim to help educators and parents alike understand a little more about the fundamental importance of the formative years.

As each chapter of the book evolves, it should be used to reflect on previous chapters, ensuring that the knowledge we acquire is applied to our existing knowledge. This is known as scaffolded learning and is achieved by connecting what we know to what we are learning.

As with any seminar I deliver, this book is designed to create discourse and discussion and should be used as a forum to share ideas and good practice. This is the foundation of any good community; the sharing of intelligent and divergent ideas in the hopes that people will challenge their own opinions and join in on the conversation. For this reason, all *Time to Think* activities in this book can be done both separately and in a group, should you wish to work with your peers through these mindful activities.

One recommendation you will find repeatedly in this book is to put your thoughts and ideas into action as quickly as possible. This doesn't mean to rush your work, but it also means don't allow your ideas to stagnate. Often our best ideas are forgotten because we get too busy, and I hope that practitioners reading this book sdevelop, grow, and create ideas that better the environment for themselves, their colleagues, and their children.

Thank you for reading!

Defining First Language

For the purpose of this book, we will use the DfES definition of first language. With an agreed-upon definition, we can hope to be on the same page as we read through the ideas in this book.

First language, often referred to as home language or L1 in the following chapters, is

> the language to which the child was initially exposed during early development and continues to use in the home and community. If a child acquires English subsequent to early development, then English is not their first language no matter how proficient in it they become.
>
> Source: School Census Preparation and Guidance for 2007
> (DfES 2007)

Defining EAL

In this book we will explore approaches to supporting the wellbeing of children raised in environments where English is used as an additional language. The first step to supporting these children in a setting is understanding how to define which children fall under the category of EAL.

EAL, like other additional needs, is a spectrum and it's up to practitioners and parents together to understand the types and degree of support required for an EAL child.

A child could be defined as EAL if he or she falls into any of the following categories;

- The child has moved to the UK from other countries where English is not the first language.
- The child has moved to the UK and is confident in English, but at home they are using a language other than English.
- The child has been born in the UK and has been exposed to English but uses another language primarily at home.
- The child is raised bilingual but primarily speaks a language other than English at home.

Top 5 EAL Myths!

1. EAL children hold foreign passports
2. EAL children have no current ability in English
3. EAL children fall into the category of SEND
4. EAL children are likely to suffer speech delays in general
5. EAL children learn languages more slowly than monolingual children

Understanding Critical Approaches to Language and Wellbeing

In this chapter, we will explore critical approaches to language development. We will explore how to think about language development in a broader capacity and how to engage with critical language theory in order to promote best practice in the early years environment.

Introduction

The importance of language is practically immeasurable. Language means different things to different people, and language represents different aspects of diverse cultures. Language can be fun, language can be misinterpreted, and language can be fiercely guarded by its speakers. Without language, our world as we know it wouldn't exist, and yet each of us unknowingly uses upwards of 16,000 words per day (Mehl et al., 2007) without paying much attention to the value of our language. This aspect of our lives, however, does not apply to everybody.

Learning Example: Ài Love You!

There exist today 1.3 billion speakers of Chinese. To most of us, this is a *foreign* language that we do not speak, understand, or read. To the Chinese, this language is a fierce tool of identity, politics, upbringing, and family history.

DOI: 10.4324/9781003190219-2

When the Chinese express love in their traditional alphabet, they do it like this:

$$愛 = \text{Love}$$

Love in traditional Chinese (pronounced Ài) is made up of a series of strokes, and typical of the traditional Chinese writing system, the character for love contains another character at its centre, the character for heart (心 – Xīn). Take a look: you can see this series of strokes right there in the middle! Now let's look at the same word in simplified Chinese, the current frontrunner for China's main system of characters:

$$爱 = \text{Love}$$

See the difference? Cantonese people certainly do. The simplified character is missing its heart, and Cantonese speakers argue that without the heart there can be no love. Something so simple has sparked much debate, and this is the nature of language.

Please note, this is not a book written with the intention of teaching its readers Chinese, but it certainly is a book that aims to show its readers the sheer importance of language, the power language has over us, and the need for educators, teachers, and practitioners of the early years to understand the effect language has on our emotional and mental wellbeing.

Language development is an important indicator for mental wellbeing in young children yet strangely, or rather fortunately for many of us, we will never truly understand the difficulties that can arise when we are unable to communicate in our daily lives.

As we practitioners of the early years go on to explore the key elements that are essential for children to learn language, it is becoming increasingly important for us to consider the key theories that support *how* children learn language. I think of this as a *back-to-basics* approach because these theories are often things we learned because we had to, not because we took any real interest. But, after gaining some experience in the setting, looking back at these theories is a great reflective activity.

None of you reading this book are expected to become academic theorists; however, we should all have a recognisable understanding of the opposing forces in language theory before we attempt to put strategies into place in the setting. When a practitioner can think theoretically, they expand their ability to think practically.

Environmentalism

With that in mind, let's think about our environment! More specifically, the potential the environment can have on a child's language development.

In 1986, Gordon Wells conducted a longitudinal study of how language develops in the family environment using observations on the *types* of language used at home. When talking with children, he found that adults often use single words (mostly nouns) in an attempt to make language easier to understand. While use of single words didn't show an effect on a child's actual language ability, it did show implications on the timeline of language development in young children. Children living in environments with rich language use enjoyed almost ten times more exposure to words and sentences than children whose families focused on more simplistic language.

This study is one of many that would suggest that the environment in which we are raised plays key a role in our language development.

Pre-dating Wells (1986), was Skinner (1957), who famously worked on conditioning experiments with rats and discovered a simple formula for behaviour:

Stimulus = Response

Skinner saw rats respond to positive and negative reinforcement and he suggested that children learn languages in the same manner. A child is first exposed to a stimulus and the child is rewarded when they use language.

LEARNING EXAMPLE

Two-year-old James is in the kitchen with his dad. He sees a pack of biscuits on the side and points to it, making a sound to indicate that he wants them. Dad sees this and says, 'What is it? You want the…'
    'Bic bics' says James.
    Dad smiles and hands James a biscuit.

In this example, the biscuit is the stimulus and the reward is being handed something to eat. The response from James's dad is what will lead James to repeat that particular behaviour and apply it to other situations. As a result of examples like this, Skinner suggests that the acquisition of language is an environmental experience. This implies that it is through interaction that language learning is enabled, and this is the foundation of Environmentalism.

Skinner (1957) also talked of the use of rewards for correct or accepted language. He suggests that it is the praise and acceptance of spoken language that reinforces use of the mother tongue.

Lev Vygotsky (1935), a pioneer in the Environmentalism movement, would further these ideas of language acquisition with the **Zone of Proximal Development (ZPD).**

Put simply, the **ZPD** is the difference in learning a child can do on their own, and the learning they can achieve with support. As a supporter of Environmentalism, Vygotsky believed that adults and more knowledgeable peers provide support to existing knowledge and language ability.

So the debate here is this: is language a product of the environment or do children have an innate ability to learn language? What do you think?

There are those within the field of language development such as Jean Piaget (1923) and Noam Chomsky (1959) who rejected the ideas of Environmentalism, suggesting its approach was oversimplified. Piaget placed emphasis on children learning for themselves through problem solving, rather than exclusively through social interaction. Chomsky believed that complex language could not be learned through simple reinforcement.

TIME TO REFLECT:

- What are your thoughts on Environmentalism?
- Do you think that the environment is more important than social interactions?
- Do you think children are capable of learning unaided by adults or do you believe like many in the Environmentalism movement that it is the environment that encourages a child to learn language?

> Have a think about certain things in the environment that could encourage child to learn language. Next, think of how you could create or expand your environment to further learning opportunities for children.

Innatism

If you aren't a fan of Environmentalism, you might just be a supporter of Innatism!

Humans are born with a set of innate abilities and traits. Two of the first to develop are fears; we fear loud noises and we fear falling. This is genetic, and we have no control over it. A Montessori teacher might say we have other innate needs such as to discover, to be independent, and to make order. These innate parts of ourselves are out of our control.

Chomsky (1964) would apply this notion to language. He describes our ability to learn and use language as a built-in device that forms part of the human brain from birth. This built-in device is appropriately named the **Language Acquisition Device (LAD)**. The LAD does not apply to any particular language, but rather is a process in the brain that allows children to learn the universal elements of *any* language.

If we look at the world through Innatism's viewpoint, the environment is not the force behind language development, but is rather the fuel that feeds an existing ability.

As with Environmentalism, there's opposition to Innatism theory. Bates and MacWhinney (1982) thought that language was a product of surrounding as opposed to an innate ability.

TIME TO REFLECT:

- Are you an Innatist?
- Do you believe that we learn language because it's already programmed into our genetics?

> In a group or on your own discussed the differences between Environmentalism and Innatism and whether these two could work together in the school setting to aid children's language development.

Social Interactionism

As the Environmentalist and Innatist separated on their core beliefs of the origins of language ability, Bruner (1960) added to the existing theories with the theory of Social Interactionism. Bruner put forward the idea that, just as a building site needs scaffolding, so too does a child need a scaffold of human interaction at home to become a competent language speaker. This scaffold of social interaction, provided mainly by family in the earliest part of a child's life, could later be removed as the child becomes a self-learning, autonomous force in their own learning journey.

Here we engage with the idea that it is through social means that language is developed, and later can be used at will by the learning child.

Emergentism

Emergentism see the positives in both Innatism and Environmentalism, and accepts that a merging of the two belief systems is likely the most realistic approach to early language development. It accepts that biologically the brain has a capability to learn language, but without external factors, what is the real power of this capability?

Fortunately, it would be wildly unethical and almost certainly illegal to put this idea to the test, but there are two key examples in our history that I implore readers of this book to look into:

* Victor of Aveyron (1788–1828), a French feral child found at the age of twelve.
* Genie (born 1957), the victim of severe neglect and abuse, raised without language.

We won't discuss these cases here as there is plenty of literature to explore related to Ginny and Victor elsewhere, but they are arguably the two richest examples of humans raised without language in our modern history.

A Note on Theories...

There is often division amongst the education community in regards to which theories or doctrines are correct. Often opinions regarding these can be quite heated, but using theory in practice is like anything we do; it should be balanced and considerate.

Theories like the ones above are there for us to explore different approaches to language development in children and what I often advise to teachers, practitioners, and parents is to try to find a happy medium of each theory.

It's not necessarily the role of a practitioner to overthink these theories, but I do implore you to take the basic information above and continue your understanding of each area. As you learn more about theories, so too will you develop an ability to use the knowledge you're gaining to be consistent in your approach to language development, and this is essential because **consistency is key!**

Being Consistent

A key consideration for any practitioner using strategies to assist children in their language development in the early years is consistency. It bears repeatingthat, when planning and strategising, say to yourself: **consistency is key!**

As practitioners, we must reinforce this idea regularly. But why do we keep telling parents and educators that consistency is key? Because it is argu-ably the first core principle of language learning.

An incredible study into the development of language in young children, the following considerations are adapted and inspired by the work of Konishi, Kanero, Freeman, Michnik Galinkoff, and Hirsh-Pasek (2014).

Children Learn What They Hear the Most

There are common misconceptions in early language development that must be debunked quickly and effectively and one of these is the negative assumption that if a child is not 'speaking' then he or she is not using language, but this is incorrect!

Laughing, crying, and singing are all sounds that exercise the muscles of the mouth and often come about because children realise very early on that making sound creates response. But infants aren't only creating sounds, they're listening too! As early as 8-months old, children begin to familiarise themselves with the regular patterns of sound in their first language. This familiarity in the first language (L1), is the basis of learning the second language (L2) from a young age, because infants are able to distinguish the irregular patterns of sound in a second language when they are exposed to it.

Put simply, when an infant is learning their first language, they are able to recognise that a second language is strange and different to the one already working away in their brain. The brain responds to this by storing the language separately, thus creating the first steps of bilingualism in a child.

But language is not just simple patterns, it is made up of syntactic structures, stresses, and tones and for children to become adept at extracting sounds in L2, large quantities of the language must be provided as early as possible.

The speech trajectory for children with high levels of exposure to language at 18 months is directly related to the ability of a child to recognise and use vocabulary in L2 by 24 months (Hurtado, Marchman, and Fernald, 2008) and this is why consistency is key.

Our brains are constantly at work to create memory, and this means that our brain has a very good system of deleting what we don't use, and language is not exempt. Adults and children alike 'forget' second languages quickly so we must expose children to rich examples of language continuously if they are to achieve fluency.

TIME TO THINK:

UK education requires almost all students to take a second language. For most of us, this was French, for others this might have been Spanish or German. No matter the language, grab a pen and a piece of paper. Now, write ten sentences about yourself in a second language that you have been exposed to.

TIME TO REFLECT:

- Did you manage ten sentences?
- Was the grammar and vocabulary correct?
- How could you have worked differently to achieve this goal?

If you managed this, then congratulations, you might just be bilingual! But if you didn't and you struggled, then you likely weren't exposed to enough language early on. But it's not too late to start now!

Exposure Rates

How much early exposure to L2 is enough? Unfortunately, this question remains largely unanswered, however early years practitioners should expect a period of silence anywhere up to six months when a child is learning a second language.

Critics of early L2 development would suggest that input from two languages may affect the vocabulary size in each individual language (Hoff et al., 2012) however the combined vocabularies of both bilinguals often match that of monolinguals. Would we call this deficit? This is down to opinion, but for most educators the consensus is that this is not a deficit.

Language learning is a lifelong journey. Native speakers still study their native languages well into their adult years and the pressure on children to 'master' second languages must be alleviated. Children will learn when they are engaged and enjoying themselves and this should be the key aim of practitioners in the early years.

Avoid TV!

There is very little evidence to suggest that television or electronic means of education are successful in providing the right level of exposure for young children. Languages are interactive entities and must be used as such!

Parents as Learning Partners

Parents must be included in the language learning process and should not be afraid to approach early years staff to learn more about language development in young children. Even if parents are not competent users of English, this does not mean they cannot assist in the learning process. Children model their behaviour on familiar adults and should see parents engaging with English.

Try This! Teachers and parents should learn and use vocabulary related to a room of the house in each other's languages, for example, encourage use of English terminology in the kitchen for a month. This can be continued with other vocabulary types too!

Creating Interest

'Language learning is enhanced when the words a child hears bear upon objects of interest.'

(Bloom, 1993)

LEARNING EXAMPLE

'My son is 3 years old and I want him to learn English. Every day, I sit him in front of the computer, and I put on videos for him to watch but he won't watch them, he keeps trying to leave the

> *computer to go do other things... how can I get him to watch the videos? I am not a teacher, and I don't know how to be fun in English.'*
>
> (Parent Seminar, Shenzhen)

TIME TO REFLECT:

- How would you have responded to this parent?
- Which strategies would you put into place to ensure this child was able to develop a keen interest in the present moment/activity?

Learning Evaluation

In terms of the learning example, it is apparent that the child in question doesn't like sitting down and watching videos, they don't interest him, and therefore he doesn't want to watch them. Parents and educators alike can find learning to be a difficult task to achieve when often parents/educators don't have a good understanding of what children like.

This is seemingly an obvious statement, and it is one that is most definitely not exclusive to language learning; children learn best when they are interested in the subject matter. Furthermore, language learning requires interaction. There is no interaction taking place when you sit a child down in front of a computer screen, so the learning process is diminished. Christakis et al. (2009) found that when the television is on, children (babies) hear 770 fewer words from a present adult per hour, leading to children spending more time in silence than in active interaction. Active interaction, we know from Ferjan-Ramirez (2017), is a key element to language learning.

Discovering Interest

Language opportunities are practically limitless, but interest is not. Children know what they like, and they welcome opportunities to share this with familiar adults. Parents and educators alike should work with this and not against it. Try not to force children into areas because they 'look good' or 'impress' other people. This will only engender boredom with the language.

From around 18 months, children are able to engage in joint attention, which is the ability for an adult and a child to share a mutual knowledge of an item, which means that adults can manipulate items to create interest in young children, thus sparking the learning of new vocabulary.

Always remember, just because an activity doesn't illicit a vocal response does not mean a child is not actively learning language.

Familiar Adults

Children model their behaviour and language on familiar adults and should see practitioners taking an interest in learning opportunities throughout the day!

Try This! Spend time with children and find common interests. Look for an enjoyable activity that provides opportunities for repetition and for development and actively engage in this in English. It's not about asking lots of questions and hoping for an answer, it's about narrating what is happening, responding with excitement, and offering the invitation to join. When a child sees an adult enjoying something, there will be a natural, curious drive to engage with this activity too.

Remember, fun can be had in any language!

Practitioners should expand on this practice by using basic sentence structures like 'Please, pass me...' or 'Let's use (colour)...'; if the child is interested and engaged then they are far more likely to start responding to the English. Use this consistently to re-enforce the structures.

Active Contexts

Reciprocal responses are a key element to the language learning process because infants and young children learn language best in active contexts.

Specifically, this means when their behaviours elicit the following responses from adults around them:

- Vocalisations
- Gestures
- Facial expressions

Children thrive on these interactions and continue to learn based on their exposure to these interactions (Tamis-LeMonda et al., 2014).

Studies conducted on English-speaking 9-month-olds showed that their ability to learn Mandarin phonemes (units of language) could only be achieved through live interaction. When the same phonemes were taught using screen-based learning, this medium proved ineffective (Kuhl et al., 2003).

A similar study of 24–30-month-olds learning verbs through both screen and active contexts showed the same levels of achievement in the children who were provided with the opportunity to learn in active contexts. Only live, socially driven interactions yielded successful results in the learning process (Roseberry, Hirsh-Pasek, and Golinkoff, 2013).

This requirement for responsiveness is not specific to one language, but rather has been found to facilitate learning across various cultures (Tamis-LeMonda et al., 2014).

TIME TO THINK:

While technology is a useful addition to the setting environment and should be utilised in settings so that children have access to a well-rounded education, there are drawbacks to having too much technology present in the learning environment. Think about the following questions in relation to technology:

1. How could you utilise technology effectively in the setting?
2. What measures could you put into place to ensure that technology is not abused in the setting?

TIME TO REFLECT:

Think about a time when you have become over-reliant on technology in the setting.

- How did this affect the flow of your teaching?
- What response did you get from the children?

Let's Co-Regulate!

Why is response/responsiveness so important? One of the answers is co-regulation, and the need for this to exist in the active context.

Co-regulation is the process by which communication between individuals is continuously modified depending on the needs of the person they are speaking to (Fogel, 1993). Put simply, conversations between speakers change constantly, and speakers need to adapt to these changes regularly during conversation.

Through co-regulation, parents and educators can consistently scaffold learning based on a child's needs. Language exchanges are often non-linear, but this non-linear nature is an advantage with scaffolded learning. Co-regulating language with a young learner is in itself an active process, requiring the attention of both speakers.

Interaction vs. Observation

It is important that parents and educators understand the clear difference between interaction and passive observation. While interactive online lessons with an educator can absolutely create learning opportunities, screen technology that has no interaction is incredibly limited in terms of its ability to teach children languages.

Label and Question

There is a clear link between early interactive parenting and later language ability and the frequency of story book reading and children's vocabulary in their L1 and L2 were also found to be related.

Try This! Educators should ask labelling questions during reading time (e.g., what is this called?). Children who experience this form of interaction are found to have greater vocabulary across their languages (Quiroz, Snow, and Zhao, 2010).

Let's Get Meaningful!

While the studies on the relationship between context and vocabulary learning are indeed limited, research into childhood development does suggest a strong correlation between learning in meaningful contexts and enriched background knowledge. (Hirsh-Pasek et al., 2009).

Han et al. conducted a study in 2011 that gives us an empirical example of how children learn through context as opposed to explicit instruction using the word 'bake'. The methods: taught through storybook and play to group one, and through storybook and explicit instruction to group two.

Subsequent tests, which followed after the groups were introduced to the vocabulary, showed that the play group, when asked to repeat the information they had gathered from the story, remembered more of the target vocabulary than the control group who were expected to perform the same task. They were able to apply the context (storybook and props) to the target language, which led to higher levels of language retention.

Children learn when they are curious and it is crucial for educators to provide environments that stimulate a child's curiosity as we provide the input that makes language learning possible (Christie and Roskos, 2006).

As language is associated with culture, as we will explore in later chapters, context also has applications on cultural understanding for children of L2. It's important for children to be provided a safe space to ask questions and learn about the culture of the language they are studying. Context is a concept I've dealt with systematically over the last seven years, and there are various methods educators can use to introduce contextual awareness to a setting:

Realia – the use of real items during play so that children can develop their language awareness along with their sensory development.

Provocations – items and activities that provide opportunities for self-directed exploration. These should usually pertain to a purport within language development.

Storybooks – A range of books with focuses on current language aspects, cultural diversity, and holistic elements linked to other areas of learning.

Discussions – circle times that provide opportunities for extended conversation and language use.

Illustrations – art work and illustrations available in settings that provide opportunities for discussion and curiosity.

A Note on Realia...

Practitioners should try at all times to use real, authentic items. For hygiene, convenience, and price, many settings provide plastic versions of an item that could be real; i.e. plastic fruit. While these items do provide play opportunities, the real version of this item provides countless opportunities for language learning. A plastic apple can be played with, but a real apple can be eaten, it can be cut, it tastes sweet, it smells earthy, it crunches when we bite it, it leaves a cool moisture on our hands; all of these are language learning opportunities.

Interest and Context

While context creation is an essential element of language and learning, don't overlook the importance of the aforementioned interest. Conversations that revolve around a child's interests pose more opportunities for retention than unbidden verbal explanations (Golinkoff, 1986). Educators should always plan contexts around the child's interest as opposed to forcing contexts on them that the adult thinks are worthy.

Reading for Context

Reading is of course an excellent method of creating context (Han et al., 2011) but it also must be followed with some form of play/activity that bridges vocabulary to experience. Children should be read to regularly and practitioners should provide contextually relevant opportunities later on to aid retention.

Remember, YouTube is not a viable alternative to reading!

LEARNING EXAMPLE

Holly is a teacher in a small kindergarten, and she teaches pre-school aged children. Holly enjoys circle time and is a capable teacher. However, Holly has noticed over the course of two months that some of her children are reluctant to speak up during circle time. She has a specific group of children who are eager to engage and at times she struggles to bring the other children into the class.

Holly requested an observation to ascertain how she might fix this problem.

During the observation, the observer noted that Holly would give up very quickly when the quieter children needed some encouragement and relied too much on the stronger children to engage with her when the circle time would lag.

This unbalanced communication was also starting to be reflected in the communication and language development of some of the children.

TIME TO THINK:

1. How could Holly have avoided this issue in the setting?
2. What are some potential solutions to rectify this issue?

TIME TO REFLECT:

- Have you experienced a situation like Holly's? How did you, as a practitioner, rectify this situation? How could you have avoided this?

D is for Diversity!

Houston and Jusczyk (2000) explored the ways in which very young children cannot distinguish between words when the gender or tone of the speaker changes, and examples of this often lead to the same concern from parents:

> 'We want the same teacher; we don't think our child will learn the language if the teacher changes!'

The rationale from parents behind this is always positive as parents want their children to form a good relationship with a single teacher. They also worry about accent changes between teachers, and how this affects language acquisition.

While the intent here is pure, the outcome often isn't. According to Richtsmeier et al. (2009), the understanding of abstract words requires exposure to multiple types of speakers. Receiving multiple input sources of a language is essential in order for children to gain a comprehensive understanding of that language.

Not only is diversity in speakers important, but also diversity in the language being spoken.

Utilising Parentese

Adults have an almost uncontrollable urge to speak to children in simplistic language due to the belief that children will struggle to understand any complex vocabulary, but this is wrong. There is a direct correlation between parents' use of rare and diverse words and a child's vocabulary range (Weizman and Snow, 2001). Therefore, parents and practitioners should incorporate broad uses of vocabulary from an early age. Diverse input doesn't just help in the development of vocabulary growth, but plays a key role in developing categorisation and concept skills, pivotal to language development, and has links to increased capabilities with later educational skills (Tabors, Snow, and Dickinson, 2001).

What practitioners should remember to use, however, is the phenomenon known as *parentese*. *Parentese* is the high-pitched tone that adults use when they are around children; put simply, we speak to children in a cute affectionate, and high-pitched tone. This is a biological drive that actually aids in the development of languages. Children are more likely to absorb language when it is presented in a high pitched, accessible range (Stern, Spieker, and Mackain, 1982). Educators, therefore, should use parentese with a range of complex vocabulary to ensure that children are developing a wide range of language skills. Virtually no relevant language is too difficult, merely our perception of how children learn is slightly askew.

Don't Dumb It Down!

Parents and educators often speak to children as if they're incapable. Words are dumbed down, sentences are said incorrectly, and topics are avoided, but children learn through exposure. Within reason, it's perfectly acceptable to introduce complicated language to children consistently.

Remember, children struggling to understand is part of the learning process!

Filling in the Gaps

Children can have very satisfying exchanges with familiar adults, and adults are very useful for 'filling in the gaps' in a child's learning (Brewer and Cutting, 2001). Parents, especially those who are practising their own L2, are often nervous to use complicated language for fear of overloading a child, however, family time is a key time for children to experience extended learning. Encourage family members to initiate and continue conversations with young children, not just Mum, Dad and the practitioner.

Holophrases!

Vocabulary is rarely used independently. Even when young children engage in single word phrases (holophrases), whole meanings are often intended. For example, when a child says 'drink' they are more likely implying 'I want a drink' or 'I am thirsty'.

When children are exposed to numerous language functions, they are able to expand their vocabulary through a method known as syntactic bootstrapping (Dionne et al., 2003). Simply put, this is the ability of young children to make inferences about language based on their existing knowledge.

Dionne et al. (2003) found that vocabulary and grammar develop simultaneously. Test results show that expressive vocabulary could be used as a predictor for grammatical knowledge. By watching and listening to children, educators and parents can note the context in which some words appear and use this to introduce new contextual clues and language functions.

Avoid Excessive Use of Flashcards

Children who are taught excessive amounts of 'flashcard vocabulary' through rote learning are unlikely to develop grammar in the reciprocal nature that is required for expressive language use. Only through real exposure is the relationship between vocabulary and grammar achieved.

Tasks for Achievement

Introduce various language functions in different contexts. As an example, use Listen and Do tasks to encourage receptive and productive language knowledge (Shintani, 2012). A listen and do task could be a baking activity, a craft, or any sort of instructional activity that the child is interested in.

Finally...

Be patient.

The reader should now have a firm understanding of how theory applies to practice in language development. Chapter 2 will explore how to apply these theories in the holistic approach.

FURTHER READING TO SUPPORT CHAPTER 1

1. Hayes, C. (2014). *Language, Literacy, and Communication in the Early Years.* St Albans: Critical Publishing.

Connecting to the Holistic Approach

In this chapter, we will explore the holistic approach, what this means, and how we can apply the holistic approach to language development specifically. Practitioners should leave this chapter with a sense of how to tie early years together in an accessible and enjoyable way.

Introduction

Holistic; don't we all love that word!

You'd be hard-pressed to find an early years setting nowadays that doesn't talk about the importance of being holistic or their strengths with the holistic approach. While I agree that many practitioners are utilising the holistic approach effectively, there has been a large number of staff I've worked with who struggle to do one thing; easily define the term *holistic*.

Do you struggle with this?

There is no shame if you do, because chances are you are using it perfectly anyway, but when we lose touch with the basics, we can begin to see misunderstandings of the roots of the holistic approach and how it applies to an inquiry-based curriculum. We need to explore the connections that are essential within the early years framework for the term 'holistic' to apply, and we need to explore how to create an enabling environment that supports multiple learning opportunities for EAL children.

DOI: 10.4324/9781003190219-3

TIME TO THINK:

In one sentence, write down a simple definition of the term *holistic*.

TIME TO REFLECT:

Did your definition use any of the following terms?

- Connected/Connection
- Interconnected/Interconnection
- The whole/Viewed as a whole
- Linked/Together

Defining Holistic

If you used some of the above terms, then we're on the right track! Holistic doesn't have to have one sole meaning, but generally, the holistic approach is all about connections. These connections can be seen on the micro-level, such as how an activity connects to a learning plan for a child, and can be seen on the macro, such as how a single activity can provide learning opportunities in every area of learning within the early years framework.

This is how practitioners should think about the holistic approach when planning and organising activities for young learners; how does planning connect each of the areas of learning within an early years framework, and furthermore, how can this be reinforced for children who do not come to a framework with English as their dominant language?

Before we tackle these challenges, let's take a look at the interconnectedness of one of our most important organs; the brain!

Connecting the Brain

The human brain is a creation of connections.

Strengthening these connections is one of the fundamental aspects of early brain development and for this reason, the first three years of a baby's life are arguably some of the most, if not **the** most, important for brain development. Every interaction, every experience is converting messy grey matter into a functioning person, and when we think about this holistically, we are thinking about the expanse of experiences, including language experiences, that we need to introduce to our little ones as they spend time in an early years setting.

Language and the Brain

While birth to three is a pivotal time for brain development, birth to ten is commonly recognised as the time in a child's life when new languages are most easily accessible source, this time period is also known as a sensitive period. The common consensus among the bilingual community is *the earlier the better*. Babies can develop bilingual brains when exposed to multiple languages, but practitioners must be diligent with the sensitive periods that children experience in order to offer the best learning opportunities. How can we as practitioners take note of this sensitivity and use it to our advantage?

When an infant is repeatedly exposed to vocabulary during the sensitive period, the brain works hard to connect some of the 100 billion neurons into a scaffold of language, this scaffold is the foundation of further learning later on in infancy.

The brain absorbs language in numerous ways:

- Casual conversation
- Songs
- Rhymes
- Reading
- Music
- Storytelling

These examples of language stimulation offer avenues to children for future interactions and learning because these interactions, both good *and* bad, affect the make-up of the connections in the brain.

If the positive connections are stimulated regularly, and in a loving and caring environment, the connections are likely to strengthen and become permanent (Graff, 2020). However, connections that are not reinforced will be subject to purging by the brain. One factor that must come under consideration here is the role that stress plays in the holistic development of a child.

Stress and Wellbeing

Toxic stress! A term we have to talk about and simultaneously need to avoid as much as possible in a setting. Toxic stress arises in particularly neglectful, abusive, or poverty-stricken situations when children are not offered adequate adult support. Stress can be seen as tolerable in a situation when a child has adults in place to support them.

For an EAL child, the stress level is potentially increased when they are removed from their familiar language and culture and how an EAL child is comforted at home is likely to differ from how a practitioner will respond to a stressful situation and this is something all practitioners need to be mindful of when recognising stress in an EAL child.

Keep in mind, however, that there are some examples of stress that are positive. The everyday challenges we all face can be seen as 'stressful', but when we are able to label these experiences as 'everyday', they take the form of learning opportunities and these are part of a child's learning journey.

How do we recognise regular stress? Easy! A child can return to a calm state in a relatively short period of time when experiencing regular, everyday stress.

How can we recognise toxic stress? This is much harder and unfortunately has more serious internal consequences than any of us can see. When a child is repeatedly exposed to physical or emotional trauma, the hormone cortisol is released. Increased levels of cortisol in the brain causes brain cell death and reduction in the connections between areas of the brain. Quite literally, the connection of the brain are damaged.

How does this connect to the holistic approach? In almost every way! When the brain is not able to form quality connections, the interconnectedness of an early years framework cannot be used effectively.

When we look at this in terms of an EAL child, the connections necessary for language learning are eradicated to such an extent that the ability of a child to develop second languages within their early years education.

TIME TO THINK:

Think of a time when you felt overwhelmed or stressed in your daily routine as an early years practitioner. Share this with others if you feel comfortable to do so.

TIME TO REFLECT:

- Was there a preventative measure to this situation?
- Do you feel your situation affected a child in your setting?
- What can you put into place to ensure this doesn't happen again?

We do activities like this to self-reflect and to become aware of our own limitations so we might be able to offer an increased level of support to the children in our care.

Holistic Wellbeing

When we support wellbeing in the early years, practitioners must look at their ability to provide support that looks at the child as a whole child. We shouldn't just take into account their educational needs but also their mental health needs, physical needs, emotional needs, social needs, language needs, and indeed, spiritual wellbeing.

Each child will have different needs from the early years and how we approach these individual needs is a core element of the approach.

Practitioners should ask questions, and talk with parents and other practitioners to learn all they can about the children in their care.

Holistic Approach to Language

How we perceive the world around us is tied to our language ability. This concept is not the easiest to understand until you begin to unravel the mysteries of a second language.

Some examples:

- When Chinese people greet each other, they don't say hello, they ask, 'Have you eaten?', an indication that the culture revolves around food.
- The Kuuk Thaayore people, an aboriginal group in Australia, do not use 'left' and 'right' as directional language, but rather see direction in terms of cardinal directions (North, South, East, West). This indicates that their language is rooted in the need for land orientation.
- Russian speakers don't have all-encompassing words for colours like blue, they must differentiate the colour based on its tone.
- Many other European languages also have masculine and feminine words, and the rule of how these are used is different in different cultures.

(Adapted from the work of Boroditsky, L., 2017. *How Language Shapes the Way We Think.*)

These language differences indicate a big difference in the abilities language provides across cultures.

These examples, and the millions more you will be able to discover on your own, are the key reason that language learning needs to be holistic. Children are not just learning language on its own, but rather are learning how to function within that language, how to view the world in that language, and how to develop within an early years framework. This connectivity is at the very heart of the holistic approach.

Language learning should allow children to make sense of the world around them rather than make sense of a chapter in a textbook. Language learning should provoke thinking and lead to further inquiries. It should be applied to, and practised in, real-life scenarios and it should have explicit connections to what children already know and can do. It should be rich with up-to-date materials easily available to children.

Isolated topics in language learning are a waste of a child's valuable time. Language should evolve as our environment evolves, and we mustn't underestimate the role of the environment in the learning of language.

Enabling Holistic Environments

An enabling environment is a space in which there is a rich and varied space for children to take safe risks. To ensure that an environment is enabling for an EAL child, ask yourself the following questions related to aspects of the environment:

On the Environment...

- Is your environment warm and welcoming?
- Does it help children to feel a sense of belonging?
- Does your environment offer a range of familiar resources?
- Does your environment offer a range of developmentally appropriate activities?
- Are there opportunities for indoor and outdoor exploration?
- Is there sufficient space for movement and collaboration?
- Are resources at the right height levels? Are they accessible?
- Is the environment too loud?

On Planning...

- Do activities serve different purposes?
- Are there developing areas of continuous provision?
- Is the environment differentiated? Are there opportunities for children to develop in different areas?

- Is the environment suitable for all children? Have you made the environment diverse and welcoming for cultural differences?
- Are there rules in place that the children understand and have collaborated on?

On People...

- Is there a place for parents in your setting to also be comfortable?
- How are you planning for individual children?
- Have you taken into account the individual interests of each child?
- How is the environment tailored to aid in communication?
- Are there sufficient rest/relaxation spaces for the children in your care?
- What choices do the children have?

Enabling EAL Environments

Enabling EAL environments also requires you to consider some of the following aspects of the setting:

- The early years environment should celebrate cultural diversity and different languages through wall displays and other resources; try displaying a welcome sign in multiple languages, including those spoken in the provision.
- Ensure that staff are familiar with the correct names of all children and parents, as well as the correct pronunciation. Don't be afraid to check this with a family before they attend.
- Use gestures, smiles, and body language to communicate straightaway.
- Provide timetables in different mediums, such as pictures as well as written words to ensure that EAL families can access this material.
- Think about familiar resources that will benefit an EAL child, and how these connect to your planning. What books do you have, dress-up clothes, toys, pictures etc. that are reflective of the entire student body?
- Use multi-modal signs (pictures and words) to highlight different activities and areas of continuous provision, these will help children to navigate the setting more easily.

- Storytime should be supported with illustrations and props to make the learning goals more accessible to EAL children.
- Host events, open days, and coffee mornings and include all families in these.
- Create opportunities for visitors to come to school that are reflective of the diverse student body, these might be musicians or language teachers.
- Try, if possible, to hire bilingual staff who can support EAL children in the setting,

In addition, for early years settings to offer a wide range of language development opportunities, they must provide children with activities, resources, and experiences that allow them to develop in English while continuing to build upon their home language in a safe environment. Environments should be reflective of the backgrounds and cultures of the children, such as:

- Dual language options for stories (audiobooks in second language also could be an option)
- Fairy tales from different cultures
- Items in the setting that positively reflect different cultures
- Instruments from a variety of countries
- Whole-world story sacks
- Ethnically diverse dolls and figures
- Celebrations of food and festivals from around the world

Final Thoughts on the Holistic Approach

As you continue to plan for your little ones, consider how the following is also incorporated into your environment and how they can be used to engage an EAL child in the setting:

1. **Physical growth** – Research and review the physical milestones your children might have. Think about motor skills, especially fine motor skills, as the monitoring of these is essential for later writing skills. Fine motor skills can be developed through small actions like using paintbrushes,

threading, digging, or playing with blocks and dough. Keep in mind the skill of *crossing the midline* and how this pertains to later access to reading and writing skills.

2. **Social skills** – Monitor and observe how your children are interacting with others. Assist with the building of social skills by connecting your child with peers and with other adults. Praise is key here, even for small actions like enjoying a snack together or taking turns.

3. **Emotional understanding** – We need to help EAL children understand how to express their emotions in a healthy and positive way. This can be achieved through *multiple* readings of storybooks, joint approaches by parents and practitioners and, most importantly, being aware of and responding to a child's needs.

4. **Intellectual development** – Children should be exposed to play as a learning tool. Children are almost constant learners and through the encouragement of active participation, we can achieve the best outcomes. Ask open-ended questions, and always encourage children to ask 'why?'

5. **Environmental understanding** – As children develop as individuals, we should also assist children in their development as global citizens. Whether EAL or not, children should grow in their understanding of the world as a whole connected unit and how they can contribute to this unit. This idea starts at home, and can develop outwards as children learn about their place in the world. Children should learn to respect their belongings, as well as those of the setting, and should further develop an idea of how to respect their environment on a macro level. As culture and values can come *into* a setting, they can also be sent home through quality education.

Environmental Audit

Being ready for any framework in the early years requires preparation and the final point we will focus on in this chapter is the benefit of an environmental audit, and how conducting these regularly can help practitioners to think and behave in accordance with the holistic approach.

When we conduct an audit, practitioners must consider that there are three main environments in the early years: the emotional environment, the indoor environment, and the outdoor environment. When practitioners implement change in these areas, it can seem a little overwhelming and maybe impossible to make any significant change in a short time frame. Practitioners should overcome this by setting priorities. Environments aren't built in a day, and indeed they are always, or should be always evolving to meet the growing needs of the child. Practitioners should set realistic time frames for change.

An environmental audit is designed in a way to provide a framework of evaluation for the current environment. Practitioners should evaluate the environment from all perspectives and assess which areas require the most improvement. Environments in the early years play a significant role in the raising of a child and without proper care and attention, can have a detrimental effect on the wellbeing of a child.

For this reason, practitioners should take time to observe the environment. Imagine, as you observe, that you are seeing it for the first time. Imagine you are a toddler or a parent; how does the environment make you feel?

Get advice from other practitioners, and work on their opinions and input, providing they're in line with your planning. A great way to encourage this as a group is to leave a camera out in the setting. Have staff and children take photos of things they love, and things they don't like. These can be used later for evaluation purposes.

 TIME TO THINK:

While it may be easy to focus by default on a child's intellectual abilities during the early years, it is equally important for a child to develop skills such as confidence, social ability, compassion, responsibility, and multiple other skills.

Create an activity/series of activities that you can use in the setting to incorporate not just one, but multiple examples of the skills listed above. Share this with your co-workers and see how they might approach the same task. Remember, you and your colleagues are also interconnected!

TIME TO REFLECT:

- How can you ensure the above activity encourages and supports language development?
- How could you share this experience with a parent so that they too might encourage language development at home?

Finally...

There is no one way for a practitioner of the early years to achieve success with the holistic approach. Follow examples, learn from your peers, and most importantly, listen to the children in your care!

The reader should now have more confidence with the holistic approach as it applies to supporting the wellbeing of EAL children. Chapter 3 will explore how our current knowledge applies to the prime areas of learning within the EYFS.

FURTHER READING TO SUPPORT CHAPTER 2

1. Siegel, D. and Payne Bryson, T. (2012). *The Whole-Brain Child: 12 Revolutionary Strategies to Nurture Your Child's Developing Mind*. London: Robinson.

Exploring the Prime Areas in EAL

In this chapter, we will explore how a child of EAL status experiences the prime area of the EYFS curriculum. We will look at specific strategies to ensure children are emotionally and socially supported, and through this support, we can hope to achieve learning goals within communication, language, and physical development. We will look specifically at the EYFS framework from the UK; however, the suggestions in this chapter are not limited to any single framework.

Introduction

There is no shame in admitting that sometimes practitioners can overlook language learning needs in the early years setting, as the common consensus nowadays is that children will simple 'pick up' new language by being exposed to it. While there is some truth to this, I'm here to tell you it's also a misconception! A good practitioner knows that this kind of thinking is limited, and doesn't take into account the scope of learning and development we expect to see from young children during their time in the early years.

EAL children, whether they are bilingual or monolingual, are involved in a number of difficult tasks. Not only processing English, but also learning the boundaries of social interactions with peers, learning to navigate the setting, and engaging with the fundamental elements of the framework in which they are being immersed in.

DOI: 10.4324/9781003190219-4

'It is evident that acquisition of linguistic knowledge and acquisition of socio-cultural knowledge are interdependent... Children develop concepts of a socio-culturally structured universe through their participation in language activities' (Ochs, 1988). For children entering a setting in which the medium of instruction is solely English, the prime areas are closely linked because the process of learning language, and learning to communicate, is highly ingrained in our ability to develop socially and emotionally.

For this reason, we will explore the prime areas as they are connected to each other and look at practices that should be put in place as children grow personally, emotionally, and within their social groups. Then we will look at the early learning goals for the prime areas.

Please remember, that regardless of what stage in the EAL process a child is, when they enter your setting, they are most likely losing access to their greatest resource – the mother tongue. This has the potential to limit the access EAL children have to support systems and learning concepts. How children are supported in this initial entry to an early years setting is an imperative aspect of our roles as early years practitioners.

Initial Support

An initial solution to this problem is having the family provide a brief home history that practitioners can use to better understand the environment from which the child is coming. This could include some information on the following:

* Primary caregiver
* Main language spoken at home
* Exposure time to English at home

Why is this information important? Once we have access to this information, we can put a number of support systems in place and we gain a baseline assessment of the existing English a child already has. For example, if a child is used to using English during mealtimes, a practitioner can use meal/snack times as a springboard for other learning. As we develop a key understanding of the initial support we can offer, so too can we form an idea of how to support the EAL child emotionally.

Emotional Support

And this is important because it could be argued that no learning can take place in the early years environment if a child does not feel personally and emotionally supported. Emotional wellbeing is the topic of much discussion; it is an indicator of academic performance, and it is one of the more delicate aspects of what we as educators take care of.

It's not only important for practitioners to anticipate and reflect on PSE issues within the EYFS, but staff must consider how EAL children develop PSE skills when their native language is missing from the setting. Children initially learn languages through play, and through social interaction (Ferjan-Ramirez, 2017) but for play and social interaction to take place, children must feel safe and supported.

 TIME TO THINK:

Take three post-it notes and write down the following:

1. Write down an experience that caused you to be significantly embarrassed.
2. Write down an experience that caused you to be considerably sad.
3. Write down an experience that caused you to feel a 'red' anger.

 TIME TO REFLECT:

Next practitioners should think about the following:

- What strategies could have been in place to prevent these situations from happening?
- Was the emotional response warranted? Remember, emotions are handled differently by each individual person.

- Is there a relatable experience that a child could go through in your care?
- What strategies can we provide to EAL children to help them cope with the same issues?

If you are completing this activity in a group, consider the following:
*Post-its should be put into the bowl and selected at random. Practitioners **should not** try to guess 'who' each situation belongs to, but they should discuss which of the three feelings they think this situation elicited: sadness, anger, or embarrassment.*

Best Practice

The purpose of reflective activities like the one above is to encourage practitioners to start thinking about how our own personal, social, and emotional wellbeing can have a detrimental effect on early years integration. As adults, we have personal strategies that we are able to put into place to help us when we feel embarrassed, but it is important to repeat that, without adequate support in place to help children to develop the same PSE awareness and strategies for coping, no learning can take place. Children must feel safe and secure if they are to develop in the early years. We must work hard to ensure that EAL children are:

- Treated equally with regard to access to the whole curriculum
- Supported in home and second language
- Valued as bilingual or monolingual speakers
- Respected equally as developing creatures

Gaining Access

Think for a moment of your daily routine, and the culture you have in your early year's setting. Due to the child-led nature of our work, the rules/systems/norms of the class are not necessarily made to be explicit. Usually, children access class culture through observing patterns of behaviour, and through access to subtle language used to direct the flow of the class.

This poses a challenge to an EAL child who has not yet developed the skills to interpret language, and so the expectation of the practitioner should be lowered to meet this need. One example of a perceived rule would be transition tools for cleaning up (e.g. clean up song) and what behaviour is expected when a child hears a language cue.

Rich Experiences

Fortunately, children are fearless explorers and to engage a child in the setting more fully, we start by providing children with a rich set of experiences. Why 'rich'? Because we need to think about the depth of knowledge and development children can receive from an experience.

TIME TO THINK:

Study the three example activities below. How would you add to/alter this activity to create a richer learning experience for an EAL child:

Activity 1 – The room leader puts sand and water tray in the corner of the room.

Activity 2 – A practitioner takes a child into the outdoor area and lets them have free play.

Activity 3 – A teaching assistant reads a book to the children in the home corner.

TIME TO REFLECT:

Write down more examples of activities you might have tried, and the success you had with these by making them more in-depth.

Personal Development

A day at school provides multiple opportunities for children to develop, and practitioners should recognise the importance of even the simplest parts of the day and the effect they can have on the personal wellbeing and development of a child with EAL.

1. Snack Time

When you have children coming from diverse backgrounds, it's highly likely you will see children bring different types of snacks. These may be from their home country, prepared at home by a family member, or bought from an international store. If this is the case, you're likely to see different languages on the packaging and you may experience different aromas and flavours to those we're used to in the UK, but the child will be comforted by familiarity. Practitioners should spend some time exploring different foods that children eat at home and encourage and engage in discussion with the whole group. When a child recognises that they're eating something different and it's appreciated and celebrated, they're likely to feel a sense of cultural belonging in the setting. To expand on this, practitioners could prepare culturally diverse snacks/meals for the children as a whole to connect children of different backgrounds to the group as a whole. This is also an excellent time for new language related to food and eating to be introduced consistently.

2. Home Corner

What makes a home? Home is a place where you're comfortable and content and there's no one way to make a home, in the same way that there is no one way to make a home corner. Children should be provided with multiple opportunities to explore different ideas related to home. This could be having decorative items that come from culturally diverse backgrounds, utensils that represent a wide range of eating habits, images of culturally diverse food, and representations of all of that within the English language. Proper labeling is a great way to start encouraging early literacy skills in conjunction with vocalisations from practitioners who are also acting as play partners in the home corner.

3. Art Time

Art and culture go hand-in-hand, and it is highly likely that children from diverse cultural backgrounds also have homes that are decorated with representations of art from their home cultures. For this reason, displays in settings should be multicultural and reflective of the child body. When we think of this in terms of scaffolded learning, it's highly likely that an EAL child is already familiar with the design, the makeup, and the colors they are exposed to in their home language. What we must do now is bridge the gap in the brain by connecting a child's existing knowledge to the English language. Art is also produced in different mediums, not just painting and drawing. Practitioners should take advantage of the multiple language and early years framework opportunities that can be in place when we approach art, using technology to capture photography and video, using our bodies to dance and move, using our voices to sing. Art provides a plethora of opportunities for language development, self-expression, and self-regulation and should never be underestimated as a resource for practitioners of the early years.

4. Music Time

This leads us into the importance of music time in the setting. Similarly to art, the music of different cultures should be explored, and children should be given access to a range of musical instruments that are native not only to the UK but to other countries. Singing also has implications for physical development. When we think of language, we don't often think of the physiological aspects associated with it, but language is a physical entity. What this means is that, like learning how to walk up steps, or hold a pencil, children are developing the musculature of their mouths as they learn how to speak English. A child whose first language is not English is likely to have different muscular development. Take for example a child of Japanese heritage; he or she will be prone to difficulties with the letters R and L as these are not prominent in the Japanese language. This is so prominent that in Japan a 'roller coaster' is called a 'jet coaster' to avoid any pronunciation difficulty. When children are given opportunities to sing, they are able to better develop the musculature needed for the English language.

5. Library

Library corners should be stocked with books that reflect the cultural dimension of the setting and could even go as far as having books in different languages, as this might be a comfort for children whose home language is represented there. Remember, supporting native language is just as important as supporting English language development. It's the role of the early years environment to make the unknown known and what better way than to have all children exposed to diverse cultural dimensions through books. Books should also be reflective of how we want children to deal with specific situations, such as conflict, stories that tell us how to deal with our emotions, and with social interaction. Library corners should also be well labeled. To encourage reading, practitioners should hold circle times or group times in the library and use the books as reference.

6. Role Play

Role play is arguably one of the most fun and inventive ways to introduce cultural diversity into a setting! Practitioners should provide opportunities for children to dress up in multicultural and diverse clothing that is reflective of the class as a whole. Quality role play could lay the foundation of a whole theme that explores cultural diversity in the setting. Palmer (2014) suggests that skilfully created role play areas lead children to develop social skills and their intonation through the mirroring of the real world. This mirroring has significant implications on the development of technical and specialist vocabulary. Something to keep in mind with role play areas is that being inventive and being high quality does not mean spending a lot of money on pre-made costumes or pre-made representations of cultural diversity. Role play comes from the mind, it comes from experience, and a child could turn a scarf into 1000 examples of cultural diversity as long as they have been provided with the framework to do so.

Top Tip for Filling the Setting with Cultural Diversity...

It's not always easy to know where to go to buy things that are culturally diverse, especially if we're not part of that community. Ask families to send things in that can be used for displays, for music, for art, and for areas of continuous provision. This is a great way to engage in parent partnership and have parents feel like they are a part of the setting too.

Unique Child

As practitioners of the early years, we are believers that children are unique. Children in your class who do not speak English as a first language already have a tangible uniqueness about them – their cultural background. Practitioners therefore have a strong starting point for the development of the child. This type of development correlates to how children come to understand who they are and what they can do. Consider the following to support the PSE development of an EAL child in your setting:

Don't underestimate the importance of relationships – children should be encouraged to play with each other, guided by familiar adults regardless of if that child speaks English or not. Practitioners should develop their awareness of the variety of communication methods at their disposal to develop a close relationship with an EAL child.

Tabors (1997) suggests that EAL children who are not taken into account may inevitably play by themselves, so much care must be taken with the social context of the EAL child in the early years.

Mindfulness for feelings and behaviour – it can be difficult to help a child develop their ability to self-regulate feelings and behaviour when that child isn't able to use English, however an introduction of mindfulness activities that can be displayed through action as opposed to words can very much help children to calm down. Something as simple as demonstrating breathing exercises could help a child to develop their understanding about self-regulation.

Response is teaching – when a child can communicate their wants and needs with us, how we respond is key to the development of the bond between child and teacher. For EAL children, how we respond is also key for their language development. Practitioners should label things for children as they're experiencing them. As an example: *'I can see that you are sad. Sad. When we cry, it's because we are sad. Can you say sad?'* This practice should be applied regularly with a range of feelings and occurrences as an EAL child goes about their daily experiences.

Encourage and celebrate independence – when a practitioner forms a close bond with a child, particularly with a child who relies on that practitioner for communication, it is possible to forget to let the child be independent. Practitioners should encourage children to be independent in the setting and should celebrate this when it happens. A child who plays even without communicating is still developing their sense of the world and their sense of the setting and this is sometimes an independent occurrence. Practitioners need to make sure that they are being mindful of the difference between an interaction and an interference.

Patience and praise – never forget that children with EAL require an incredible amount of patience. There is an expected time frame of up to six months in which an EAL child will remain quiet as they are absorbing and learning how to use the English language. Just because the child is not speaking does not mean that he or she is not acquiring language and developing their language skills. Practitioners should be patient with this time frame and be patient with the child. All positive behaviour should be praised, and practitioners must make sure not to punish children when they make mistakes in the English language; this will only foster an environment of fear of language. Remember, all uses of English from an EAL child are a positive occurrence and should be treated as such.

Critical Reflection

The EYFS is based on a stages-not-ages approach in the sense that every child develops at a different rate. Observation is a practitioner's best friend. If you have an EAL child in your setting under your care, it is essential to observe how the child responds to receptive language. Can the child follow instructions? Can the child point to objects when you name them? Can the child follow some form of routine when it's vocalised?

If a child is showing no development of their receptive skills, then this is a major concern. Without the development of receptive skills, children are likely to struggle in their social relationships, their spoken language, and their general development. If a child in your care shows no development of receptive language skills within the period of six months, the best solution to this is a referral to a speech therapist as there could be another underlying issue contributing to the delay.

Becoming a Social Butterfly

The first bond we expect to see from a child is the bond with a practitioner. If your setting uses the key person system then it's likely the child will bond with that key person, though in practice, this isn't always the case. Being away from a primary caregiver can be a difficult transition for any child, but keep in mind that for an EAL child this means that they're also away from their primary language and primary means of communication. Having a strong bond with a key practitioner is the first step for an EAL child to develop their social communication skills.

As children are supported in their personal development, you will see a natural link to their development as social beings. Practitioners should see an upwards gradient in communication, and confidence to engage in social situations. The most obvious examples of these would be seeing a child begin to interact with familiar and unfamiliar adults or interacting with other children in the setting. As we've explored key elements to PSE development, so can we look at social interaction and its effect on the second prime area of the EYFS, Communication and Language.

Critical Reflection

The nature of language acquisition is clearly a pressing concern for those practitioners involved in the care of an EAL child. Staff in settings should regularly discuss who is best to support EAL children. Practitioners should not feel afraid to voice their concerns in supporting a child who is EAL. Only when we feel able and supported ourselves can we properly support an EAL child. This support is an intricate part of their social development and their communication development, and so should always be taken seriously.

TIME TO THINK:

Discuss with a colleague, or with a group of colleagues, a time when you have struggled with the development of a child's social skills. Write down some key reasons you believe this child struggled with social skill development and share these with others. Alternatively, research solutions to best meet the needs of your own practice.

TIME TO REFLECT:

- What strategies could be put in place to prevent issues with social skill development?
- Will these strategies support an EAL child?

Social Scaffolds

Play in all its forms is an important vehicle of learning for young children, and like any skill, children must develop skills to play alongside one another. Social skills, like all skills in an early years framework, cannot just be linked to a singular learning goal. Social skill development also plays a key role in other emerging skills such as empathy, confidence, and self-regulation. How we navigate children through these social scaffolds is largely down to the planning cycle (observe, assess, plan) and how we apply this cycle to each unique child. Let's look at some key ways to support these scaffolds in the setting, and how these can be tailored to support children with developing communication and language skills.

Structured Activities Provide Opportunities for Social Interaction

Structure! A word we try to avoid if possible in the early years as we navigate the play-based, constructivist, and child-led approach. But sometimes, when we say structure, we don't mean forcing children into strict routines; we can mean:

- Providing equipment and materials that require cooperation or sharing
- Focusing activities in a limited number of areas to encourage social interaction
- Partnering with children in their play to hand out particular roles to children

Model Social Behaviour

Children will follow in the footsteps of familiar adults and should see the adults in a setting engaging in the same behaviours that are expected of them; for example:

- Demonstrating attention-getting cues such as raising a hand, saying 'excuse me', etc.
- Demonstrating appropriate conversations
- Inviting children to play with you and have children copy this invitation
- Using language associated with social behaviour such as sharing, caring, turn-taking, helping others, etc.

Teachable Moments

Circle Time is usually the most structured part of the early years routine and is the perfect time to have children reach a consensus about the rules of the setting and the effects of our behaviour. When children hear correct termi-nology, such as generosity, sharing, and tolerance, they are more likely have a better context for what they're seeing in their daily routines:

- Teach proper use of manners, such as how to get someone's attention.
- Teach that if I am nervous, I can smile or nod at somebody instead of speaking.
- Rehearse social skills with new sentence structures.
- Show children how to give and accept compliments.

Specific Language Abilities

Whilst children are developing their general language abilities and com-munication skills, it's also important to develop specific language abilities such as:

- expressing views and opinions
- responding to ideas
- negotiating with peers
- expressing how we feel
- expressing cause and effect of feelings

TIME TO REFLECT:

- Have you used any of these suggestions before?
- What were your successes?
- What were your failures?
- How can practitioners better prepare their environments for this?

Being Collaborative

Collaborative work and play is the natural outcome when children develop their social abilities, social understanding, and communication skills. This collaboration provides some of the richest examples of language development in a developing EAL child. Language used in these interactions is often intricate and complex as children learn to negotiate, respond, and resolve specific situations. Let's look at specific instances in which we can support collaborative play.

Foster children's social interactions by drawing attention to and showing interest in what other children are doing, playing with, and producing. Ask an EAL child what they think of someone else's work. Would they like to join in? Would they like to do a similar piece of work?

Encourage children to use their social skills directly, such as encouraging a child to ask their friend for a piece of paper. Providing cues is a great way to get children thinking collaboratively. It should be noted, however, that this method should be used only in organic and naturally occurring situations, and not forced on children. Research shows that children who are regularly forced to engage in social interactions grow to develop an inhibited sense of social awareness. When the social interactions are forced, they are known as 'directive'; these should not be used unless initiated by the child themselves.

Make note of social interactions using sociograms and use these social interactions to encourage further interactions as you plan for each week. If a child shows interest yet reluctance to engage in a social interaction, this is a great time to try to work on their confidence skills. Sociograms are a fantastic way of tracking a child's social behaviours at school as we can literally see how children are interacting with each other, who they interact with most frequently, and what the content of these interactions is. Sociograms are an excellent and quick addition to any learner's profile.

Help children to understand the meaning behind social behaviours such as reasons for conflict in the class, reasons other children might feel upset, and also reasons we may be happy and joyful in school. Guide children through social interactions and prime them with ideas of how they might respond.

Encourage kindness not just by saying 'be nice' or 'say sorry' but by exploring ways we can be kind to each other, and ways we can hurt others when we're not being kind. Practitioners should discuss 'good choices' and what these mean in order to support the development of healthy social skills, and the development of rich communication skills.

Learning to Listen

When a child is developing their communication skills, a critical mistake that parents and practitioners can make is focusing too heavily on the expressive skills as evidence of language learning. The expressive skills encompass writing and speaking, areas that provide empirical evidence that children are able to use language. However, as previously discussed in this chapter, receptive skills are just as important, and children not only need to learn how to listen, but must be consistently developing their receptive skills.

This does not mean learning how to follow instructions or learning how to be well behaved in the old-fashioned meaning of the term, but it does mean learning how to take in language that has quality meaning.

Critical Reflection

Practitioners should always be considering the difference between 'hearing' language and 'listening' to language.

Listening Purposes

Listening serves a purpose both for language development and for understanding language itself. These can be:

- Identifying the purpose of an item or activity
- Detecting meaning of nuanced language
- Understanding emotional undertones in language
- Differentiating fact from fiction
- Identifying descriptive vocabulary

Hayes (2016) points out the children should not just be given opportunities to listen to language, but practitioners should also indicate what children should be listening for. As children develop the ability to decode language and understand meaning, so too can they use it as a tool for their development.

Being Emotional

Gaertner et al. (2008) studied the harmful effects of negative emotionality on a child's ability to focus. This study found that increased periods of distress had a significantly detrimental effect on a child's time in the learning environment.

Research indicates that children who are mentally healthy tend to be happier, show greater motivation to learn, have a more positive attitude towards school, more eagerly participate in-class activities, and demonstrate higher academic performance than less mentally healthy peers (Hyson 2004). Children who exhibit social and emotional difficulties tend to have trouble following directions and participating in learning activities compared with their mentally healthier/mentally supported peers. Children who suffer heightened emotional stress may be more likely to suffer rejection by classmates, have low self-esteem, and do poorly in school.

Children who are socially and emotionally healthy tend to demonstrate and continue to develop several important behaviours and skills (McClellan and Katz, 2001), and while it's not always easy to determine the emotional wellbeing of a child, answering the following questions can give you a broader idea of the wellbeing of a child:

- Would you describe the child as generally in a positive mood?
- Does the child listen to and follow directions?
- Can you think of examples of close relationships that the child has?
- Is the child regularly showing interest in others?
- Have you seen evidence that the child is able to regulate their own emotions? (for example the child might sit in the library when upset)
- Can you observe examples of non-verbal communication?
- Can you observe examples of the child playing with others?
- How does the child in your care resolve conflict with others?

As you answer these questions you are already beginning to develop a key understanding of the emotional needs of an EAL child. Establishing this trusting relationship is paramount to the education that will take place in the setting. How can you as a practitioner continue to support this trusting relationship with an EAL child?

Show warmth and affection consistently – even on bad days when children aren't doing what you want them to do, warmth and affection are critical to a child's wellbeing (Ostrosky and Jung 2005). For an EAL child, warmth and affection should be shown through non-verbal communication, through kind gestures of help, through tactile means, and with assistance for that child.

Respect and care about every child – when we show children that we are listening to them and understanding their feelings, wants, needs, and desires, we are showing that we respect the positive relationship that is developing between us and them. As this relationship develops, children will feel more confident and competent to explore and learn (Dombro, Jablon, and Stetson, 2011).

Teach emotional skills intentionally – children should be exposed to literature that discusses solutions to our emotional states and how we can address these with in-the-moment strategies. Take as an example the book *When Sophie Gets Angry* by Molly Bang; this book explores the anger felt by a little girl named Sophie and how she uses nature and reflection time to calm herself down. Books like this are excellent for EAL children because they introduce key vocabulary and visual learning aids simultaneously. Consider ways to introduce emotions to a child who doesn't understand the language you're using i.e., stomping on the floor to demonstrate anger.

Plan follow-up activities – there's little benefit to a child when exposed to language uses once or twice, there must be consistency in order for language to develop. For these strategies to work, practitioners should plan follow-up activities such as arts and crafts, games, and singing time to encourage the simultaneous development of language and emotional awareness.

Let the children be observers – children learn through the observation of familiar adults, and whilst observing, a child is developing ideas about how new behaviours are formed, and these ideas are a tool to self-guide their own actions (Bandura, 1977).

Giving cues – teachers in the early years (and beyond) should avoid at all costs shouting, yelling, or being aggressive with children. Practitioners should develop cues that help EAL children understand that their behaviour requires change in a given situation. Consider moving closer to children as a non-verbal cue, or consider gently placing a hand on a child's hand to redirect their attention and behaviour. Consider also highlighting other areas in the setting that children could go play with and guiding them away from a negative situation.

Coaching on the Spot

A day in the life of an early years teacher is often very rapid and can naturally be forgotten by a busy practitioner. Important moments can be overlooked when a practitioner doesn't have the time to make an observation, but just as we expect children to reflect, so too must practitioners take the time to be reflective in the moment. *Coaching on the Spot* is an excellent method of helping children to develop their emotional awareness, it's also an excellent way to introduce key vocabulary consistently to a child with the EAL. Coaching on the spot involves working through several stages and identifying with the outcome of each of those stages:

1. I am listening with full attention and restating what children say to me.
2. I am stating how I think you feel and seeing if you respond. (This exposes children to more vocabulary.)
3. I see if you can repeat what I have said to you, but I don't force this to happen.
4. I accept and reflect your feelings and I'm actively listening to you.
5. I hope you understand that how you feel is normal and sometimes we all feel the same way you feel now.
6. I will provide you with examples of how I feel, and also tell you how I think we can solve the problem together.
7. I'm happy for you to stay with me or for you to self-comfort if I think you need some alone time.
8. I will not put you in isolation for having feelings, and I will not label you negatively as you try to work through your feelings to a positive outcome.

TIME TO THINK:

Have a look at the list of common behaviours below. Action plan how you might put a strategy in place to work through these behaviours with an EAL child.

1. The child constantly refuses to share.
2. The child is regularly disruptive when other children are engaged in a group activity.
3. The child often resorts to being physical with other children when they don't get their own way.
4. The child gets very upset during transition times in the setting.
5. The child refuses to engage in circle time and will wander around the room when you try any activities.
6. The child uses boisterous behaviours during art and craft time to just make lots of mess and destruction.

TIME TO REFLECT:

- Did any of your colleagues have similar strategies?
- Have you seen successes or failures with specific strategies before?
- How could you fix this?

Key Support Strategies for EAL Children

Peer groups – EAL children need access to consistent good models of language not just from adults, but also from their peers in the setting. Children are more likely to have successes in their language development when playing alongside children who either have English as a first language, or who have higher proficiency in English than the child in question.

Embrace bilingualism – EAL children require a standard of conceptual development as they are learning English and in many cases, we can rely on their mother tongue to provide these concepts. Children require opportunities to hear and use a large variety of language, and as a child becomes secure in their mother tongue, they create a bridge to their second language. Talk with parents regularly about a child's development in L1 in order to better understand how a child is developing overall.

Context is key – Practitioners must always take careful consideration of the contexts in which they are introducing language. When a task is introduced through the medium of a relevant and rich context, language tasks are more easily accessed by the child. To ensure your contexts are relevant, ensure that children are engaging in scaffolded learning, building on their previous experiences, and most importantly, being exposed to language that is relevant to the situation they are in at the present moment.

Exploring the Prime Early Learning Goals (Communication and Language)

Finally, let's explore key things to look for within the prime early learning goals of the EYFS that may aid in your work with an EAL child.

Listening, Attention, and Understanding

The children in your care should be seen accepting praise and using their body language to communicate. As we've discussed, body language is largely responsible for how our communication is received and how we register this form of communication from children will give us insight into their understanding. If children are nodding, shaking heads, pointing, waving, stamping feet, these are all methods of communication that show evidence of the early learning goal.

Practitioners should utilise visual aids, real objects, body language, facial expressions, songs, and repetition in order to help children understand more English even if they're not expressing it verbally. In most instances, visual aid or a real object will be your best friend in helping a child to understand what's happening.

Speaking

The silent period for an EAL child is a time frame of around six months and during this period you can expect minimal English from the child in your care. This is normal to experience. However, there are some easy methods you can use to elicit spoken language from children:

- **Choral drilling** – have the entire group of children repeat a sentence or phrase.
- **Individual drilling** – have the target child repeat a sentence or phrase.
- **Echoing** – repeat the things children say to you and give them more complex structures to stay back.
- **Give choices** – this will elicit a response, as the child will want to make a choice (between a car or truck, for example).
- **Model sentences** – model the language you expect to see; if a child says pencil, you can say the red pencil.
- **Use statements** – an important aspect of real development is to not overwhelm a child with the questions but use simple statements that they too can use later on.
- **Praise** – and praise every use of language even if it's in the home language; this will encourage expressive language development.

Exploring the Prime Early Learning Goals (PSE)

Self-Regulation

Being self-aware links into the cultural aspect of the EAL child because often when a child first enters a setting, there won't be elements of their home culture available to them and a child will likely become quite nervous because of this. This in itself is a type of self-awareness; the child recognises they've been removed from their language and culture.

As practitioners we can combat this by making sure that there are things in the setting that encourage a child to be confident and aware that their culture is just as important, and their language is just as important as English. This can be done through:

- Pictures/photos from child's home
- Toys that represent different cultural backgrounds and ethnicities
- Artwork that represents diverse cultures
- Multi-language labels

Managing Self

Feelings and behaviour can be a particular challenge for a practitioner to engage with, with an EAL child, and the first aspect of this that practitioners should consider is the word 'managing'.

We use this term often in contexts for feelings and behaviour, but it's important that practitioners remove this term from their educational practices; there's no way to manage someone's feelings and behaviour. We can only help a child understand their feelings and behaviour and attempt to reach a more positive outcome.

To achieve this for an EAL child who might not be able to talk about their feelings, settings should employ:

- Visual representations of feelings at all times in the setting, which could include pictures on the wall that the child has access to
- Portable feelings cards such as 'Feeling Sticks' that they can take out whenever there is a communication breakdown
- Practitioners should also rely on parents to discuss feelings in the home environment so that children know how best to cope with these issues in the setting.

Remember; representations should always be followed with vocalisations so that the child is learning how to communicate. This will lead to more positive outcomes.

Building Relationships

Start by observing the interactions a child has with other children. What type of communication methods do the children use with each other? For example, does the EAL child use non-verbal means, whereas the English-speaking child uses verbal means to communicate?

Encourage social skills by then engaging in the play, helping to bridge communication between both children. But ensure your interaction is not an interference.

Practitioners could interact by:

- Providing extra toys or provocations
- Talking about sharing

- Initiating a group activity by having jigsaws or puzzles to complete
- Calling on more confident children to assist EAL children during circle times

Exploring the Prime Early Learning Goals (Physical Development)

Gross Motor

Fortunately, physical development relies primarily on using our bodies so practitioners and their EAL children can take some respite from thinking too much about English language development.

However, practitioners do have an opportunity to take advantage of physical movement to help children develop their language skills, and we can do this holistically using songs and dances to encourage EAL children.

Furthermore, practitioners should be active with the children in their care. With an EAL child, practitioners should make quality use of expressive language during movement time. provide commentary to children as they are engaging in their gross motor skill development, and use this to springboard to other language functions.

When children are moving, their brain is connecting their learning potential to their movements, which will help to fortify the language development in their brain.

Fine Motor

Unlike gross motor, fine motor skills are absolutely indicative of language development because our fine motor skills include our ability to write. To support fine motor development, practitioners should think about:

- Threading/lacing activities
- Use of tools and manipulatives
- Playdough
- Food play

- Use of large tools like paintbrushes
- Use of pencils/crayons for mark-making

Once it's appropriate to do so, practitioners can introduce written alphabet form, which will in turn help children to practise the physiological movement of the mouth related to the English alphabet, and to develop increased literacy skills.

Finally...

Ensure that the children in your care are loved and supported emotionally, and the rest will follow as you grow and develop a bond with them.

The reader should now have more confidence in approaching the prime areas of learning within the EYFS framework. Chapter 4 will explore how to continue working through the framework within the specific areas of learning.

FURTHER READING TO SUPPORT CHAPTER 3

1. Langston, A. (2019). *Evaluating Early Years Practice in Your School*. London: Bloomsbury.

Exploring the Specific Areas in EAL

In this chapter, we will explore the specific areas of the EYFS curriculum:

1. Literacy
2. Mathematics
3. Understanding the World
4. Expressive Art & Design

We will explore methods of support, strategic planning, and scaffolded learning to encourage EAL students to engage with the specific areas of the curriculum. We will look specifically at the EYFS framework from the UK, however the suggestions in this chapter are not limited to any single framework.

Introduction

Julia Child once famously said that we must have the 'courage of our convictions' when attempting a difficult task, and there can be some difficulty for children when approaching the specific areas of learning within the EYFS. The specific areas give our little ones the chance to explore all of the creativity and wonder of the world, but they also pose challenges in reading ability, mathematical cognition, and fine motor development, and of course, language ability. Our children need to be courageous when approaching these challenges, but so too do our practitioners need to have the courage of their convictions when bringing a host of activities and opportunities to a class with mixed-language children.

DOI: 10.4324/9781003190219-5

The early years framework itself provides excellent opportunities for practitioners to engage in continuous development with each other when planning for the education of children with EAL status. Practitioners should:

- Be aware that being EAL is not a deficit but an asset, as our first languages play a huge part in our identity, and our learning of other languages.
- Have high expectations of EAL children in terms of cognitive challenges which should be kept at an appropriate level throughout a child's development.
- Support differentiated planning that provides access to the EYFS framework.
- View language development not only as a means to communicate, but as a foundational skill that supports all learning.

Planning

Settings are presented with two main tasks when working with an EAL child: developing the use of English, and developing the child within an early years framework. Our role is to ensure a child reaches their full potential, and how we plan for this is directly linked to the outcomes children will reach. Within the early years, there's no single way to plan for your children. Practitioners can plan using:

- **Thematic approach** (learning through specific topic focuses in which elements of the EYFS are intertwined)
- **Long-term planning** (planning for a particular strategic goal throughout an extended period of time)
- **Medium-term planning** (planning for extended periods of time up to 6 weeks)
- **Weekly planning** (specifically focusing on how the learning environment will develop on a weekly basis)
- **In-the-moment planning** (allow the children to lead the planning and write up as it happens, provide further opportunities as you see needs in development)

Usually within the early years, we try to avoid long term planning unless a child has a specific additional need such as a behavioural issue, and the reason for this is that it stifles the child-led nature of the EYFS if we have a constant need for children to follow our lead, as opposed to us following theirs.

In-the-moment planning is currently incredibly popular with early years frameworks; however, when a child with EAL is in need of structured support, a practitioner must be cognisant of how other types of planning and assessment are being utilised to maximise the language learning opportunities for this child.

Practitioners should keep in the mind the following when planning:

- The context for learning is relevant, and creates an intrinsic motivation for the child.
- There is cultural inclusivity and a celebration of cultural diversity.
- There is a whole school/whole class approach, and children of all backgrounds and needs are included.
- Support is put in place for the specific language needs of the task.
- There are opportunities provided for children to be active in their language use (singing, speaking, listening, playing)
- The role of each adult is made clear, and adults plan for and know the difference between interactions and interferences.

When planning, practitioners must pay special attention to the inclusivity of the activities at hand. Language development should be encouraged *within* a curriculum as much as possible, as research shows that time out of class spent focusing on language tuition is actually detrimental to how a child develops within the framework.

Exploring Literacy

All languages consist of four key elements, and these are reading, writing, listening, and speaking. These four elements can be further broken down into two categories: passive language and active language.

Can you guess the difference between active uses of language and passive uses of language?

TIME TO THINK:

Take a look around the room you're in. Consider the following;

- What can you see on the walls?
- Are there signs telling you where to go?
- Are there books on the bookshelves?
- Is there a tv? Does it have subtitles on?
- Is language written in your native language?

If the language you see is in your mother tongue, you will have no control over your reading ability, your brain has decided for you to take in the information. This is a passive use of language. However, if you are driving to a new location, you are likely searching for information, road signs, landmarks etc. This is an active use of language.

Unlike reading, we are often able to switch off our listening ability, tuning out spoken language that we don't want to hear. Even though we can hear noise, we often will be able to ignore the content if it doesn't interest us.

Now imagine that the signs you see aren't English. They're in a foreign language that your brain can't decipher. Maybe you can read the phonetics, but you can't understand the meaning of the sounds.

What planning can we put in place to support a child who is immersed in a language environment that they cannot access?

TIME TO REFLECT:

This issue does not just affect children, many languages use a system of writing that is not as easily recognisable as the Roman alphabet. While many families may speak English, spoken language and read language are not necessarily developed simultaneously, and even advanced speakers may have difficulties with literacy skills.

> How can we as practitioners develop literacy skills with EAL children? And how can this be filtered back into the family unit?

Triggers for Language

Literacy skills are not only crucial in order for children to develop reading and writing skills, but also to assist children in developing the power of response. Literacy acts as a literal trigger for language use (Wells, 2009). As children learn to read, they are more likely to initiate conversation, more likely to understand situations, and more likely to achieve goals in their second language. For this reason, we will engage with the area of Literacy, and discover how this area of learning can support the other areas.

With literacy boasting such an important role in our language development, practitioners cannot only consider how to work on the development of literacy skills, but must also consider the importance of *interest*.

Creating interest is no easy task, but Cambourne (1988) produced a theory of the fundamental elements that must be present in the daily life of a child in order for interest and skill development to be seen. Since these elements arguably can be applied to other areas of language development, we will explore these in detail, with some handy tips of how to achieve each one. As you read, reflect on how each of these can be utilised in your setting. The following list is an adaptation of the work of Cambourne (1988).

1. Immersion

Immersion is the idea that for a child to gain the ability to read, then that child must be surrounded by printed language throughout the day. The immersive language approach (being surrounded by the target language for extended periods) is well documented and is often desired by those wishing to learn quickly and effectively. When children see words all around them, there is an intrinsic motivation to decode language, along with an extrinsic need to know what this information means.

How can we achieve immersion?

Classrooms and settings should have displays up that reflect the learning taking place in the setting. Remember, consistency is key in language development and children should see visual representation of both pictures and words of contextually relevant language i.e. things being discussed in your thematic approach. If you are exploring animals, there should be animal displays on the board and all displays should be accompanied with language use.

Consider producing a 'Little Artist' gallery in your school or setting whereby children can verbalise the background and intent of their creations. These verbalisations should be written down in conjunction with children, with practitioners helping children to formalise language, and engage with their own words in a written form. This idea could then be expanded out to other projects/learning opportunities whereby children are not just surrounded by language but are surrounded by *their* language.

Further, labels are important and should be used for all resources. Consider how you read these and demonstrate these to children. When we read out labels, we should focus on the phonetic makeup of sounds and have children try to imitate. As children see language being used, they're more likely to engage with the language they see independently. This leads us into the second fundamental aspect of learning to read: demonstration.

2. Demonstration

Children see adults as models of behaviour. Often when we are interested in something a child will take an interest too and this is a key element of the curiosity approach; adults must show an interest too. Children should see adults making sense of the words around them and utilising words to achieve tasks.

How can we achieve this?

First try to incorporate activities that require the following of instructions. Always have a printed copy of instructions read on a series of flashcards so that children can relate to the context of the situation. Read these out and ask concept check questions. A concept check question, or CCQ, is a question we ask young learners to ensure they understand what we're going to do. When we demonstrate the reading of an instruction and then ask questions, we are demonstrating to a child that we need written language to understand the nature of the task at hand.

Another method of demonstration that actively involves the child is to pretend to experience difficulty with written words and ask children to assist with the reading. Practitioners and children can sound out words together and then check on the meaning of those words as they read. This will help children to develop their decoding skills (sounding out words), and start to understand that written words have meaning and these meanings already exist in their brains. As EAL children develop in the early years, they're developing vocabulary, so often a child will understand meaning, and we bridge that gap by supporting reading ability. As we do this, we are already encouraging a child's confidence to engage!

3. Engagement

We hope to see engagement across all aspects of the early years as we want children to be engaged with the process of an activity or in an area of learning. Early years has always been concerned with process over product and literacy is no different. Within the engagement aspect of literacy, we hope to see children take interest and then try to emulate what they hear and observe.

How can we achieve this?

Ensure your school is utilising an evidence-based phonics program such as Jolly Phonics, Letters & Sounds, or Oxford Owl, that children can engage with on a weekly basis. Literacy needs consistency just as much as any other element of language development, so it's important for children to be engaged in some form of evidence-based literacy activities every week.

Another method of engagement might be to send home *home-learning* opportunities for parents to try. A child's learning environment does not stop when they leave a setting and it is essential that parents are also taking part in their child's education. Parents should let practitioners know which books children like to read at home and children should be encouraged to do a show and tell activity with these books. This will encourage children to engage with stories more closely, even if they can't yet read. A child with access to language opportunities can still very much become a gifted storyteller.

4. Expectation

When parents and practitioners work together in this way, an expectation is created that the child will learn to read. If you, like many practitioners, believe that children should be respected in their own right as young learners, you will also explain this expectation to the children you are working with.

I believe in the mantra that if a child is mature enough to ask a question, then they are mature enough to hear the answer and I believe that this applies to our expectations of children. If we have an expectation of a child to learn how to read, then the child should be aware of this expectation and know that when we teach them letters and sounds, we have an expectation of where this skill will lead them.

How can we achieve this?

Familiar adults could share stories about learning how to read in circle time. Within the holistic approach this would also feed well into PSE development so children can hear about the difficulties that come when we learn to read. Adults can reference popular materials that children might be already engaged with and explain the endless opportunities once we learn how to decode these materials.

Practitioners should also think outside of the box when introducing literacy activities to young children. It's very common that when practitioners try to teach literacy skills, they focus only on books, pens, pencils, and paper. Teacher should utilise other methods to encourage fine motor development and phonics understanding such as:

- Expressive art
- Craft materials
- Manipulatives such as playdough
- Messy play/messy bags
- Name stations

5. Responsibility

As with all early years approaches it is important that children feel a level of autonomy over their reading development. Early years frameworks such as Reggio Emilia, Montessori, Te Whariki, and the EYFS encourage practitioners to allow children to direct their own learning while adults act as a play partner in the setting. This idea is in keeping with some of our key theories from Chapter 1; children learn what they are most interested in and the same applies to literacy development. As we observed children in the learning environment, it is important to note which elements of literacy children are engaged with and use that as a starting point; this allows children to take responsibility for the learning process they are undertaking.

But how can we achieve this with a child whose first language is not English?

It's important for settings to remember that children need to be immersed in language in order to learn how to read, but this language doesn't necessarily need to be English to start with. By allowing children to have books and resources in their native language, we can give them the responsibility of learning how to translate these into the second language, English. Think about incorporating the following ideas into your practice:

- Have children pick the books they want to read. Consider creating a book monitor system so that children know who is responsible for the learning environment during which weeks.
- Encourage parent partnership by having parents join a library system at your school. Many early years settings are in areas that would be considered deprived, and not all families can afford the same resources at home. When a setting opens a learning library that is open to families, reading at home is more likely to take place.

6. Approximation

The next key element of reading is approximation, and this may be the most controversial element in the group because there are many discussions on how we interact with children when we teach literacy skills.

Approximation in literacy skills is the theory that when we talk, we allow speakers to make copious mistakes. Many people from the UK have different accents, and we use dialects that are localised to the area we were raised in. Even when we make mistakes in spoken language, it's still easy for us to understand one another, however, this same rule does not apply to reading. When we see a child reading words, some practitioners would argue that we must expect accuracy and make little allowance for errors in reading.

This is a double-edged approach because the very nature of the early years environment is to allow children to take risks, however, when we think of reading skills there are rules; there is a set format to the alphabet and a set way that those letters link to one another and can be used. Children should be encouraged to explore with literacy to an extent but praising serious mistakes could lead to teachers needing to fix these mistakes at a much later date.

This is especially crucial for children who are learning English as a second language because these children may already be familiar with their native alphabets and their native pronunciation.

TIME TO THINK:

Practitioners have to understand the difference between what constitutes an interaction and what constitutes an interference.

Write down what you consider to be the difference between these terms.

TIME TO REFLECT:

There will be times in the day for all practitioners when they mistake the difference between an interaction and an interference. An interaction should always be something that continues/adds to the learning environment. Children should be asked relevant questions, should be encouraged to continue taking risks, and they should at all times be expected to engage on a level that is appropriate to them. This is an interaction. However, when a practitioner asks excessive questions, or pushes a child to do something that they aren't ready for, or stops a learning moment from occurring, this is interference. We aren't actually enabling the environment when we do this but creating an environment where a child is likely to withdraw from learning.

7. Use

Well, practice makes perfect! Children should be exposed to proper example of letters and sounds regularly and should be encouraged to take part once they are confident and able to do so. Literacy, like the other areas of learning, should not exist on its own in the course of the daily routine but should be used effectively in partnership with other areas.

Although many of us have forgotten the importance of mouth movement when we are speaking, we must remember that second languages take a toll on the muscles of the mouth. Languages are a physiological thing and require the same practice as learning how to lift weights. As children practise and use literacy skills, so too are they working on their musculature.

How can we achieve this?

- Provocations – there should be multiple opportunities for children to work on their writing skills during their free playtime.
- Find and write – children should be given the opportunity to find their own name and practise writing this out.
- Word hunts – children should be set to task to find and recognise specific word groups throughout their time in the setting.
- Story circles – children should be read to regularly with the use of props, and children should also be asked to read to others. Even if a child does not understand the words, they can engage in imaginative story telling.

LEARNING EXAMPLE

Laryssa is the early years teacher for a school using the EYFS, with influence from Reggio Emilia. Every day Laryssa has the children choose a letter from a box and she challenges them for morning exercise to lie down on mats on the floor and recreate the letter with their bodies. Laryssa takes photos as she does this. By the end of the first month, Laryssa has enough photos to recreate the entire alphabet and she does so on a display board as she teaches letters and sounds. Throughout the course of the year, Laryssa recreates the entire alphabet on a display board using the children's photographs.

TIME TO THINK:

* Do you think Laryssa's literary idea is a positive addition to the class?
* How could this activity encourage children to be invested in literacy?
* How would you have approached this activity? Would you have edited it in some way?

TIME TO REFLECT:

* What could have gone wrong with this activity?
* Have you tried something similar and had any success?
* Could you use a similar activity for other areas of learning?

8. Response and Feedback

The final element is response and feedback, and let's be honest, we all enjoy a compliment! Practitioners should ensure that quality feedback is incorporated into their teaching practice. Children need to hear praise in the following situations:

- When they get an answer correct.
- When they try and fail.
- When they read unassisted and unaided.
- When they take an interest in the reading corner.
- When they spontaneously call out letters and sounds they can see.
- When they recognise that a word begins with a specific sound.

When we celebrate and encourage even the smallest successes, children will find a vested interest in trying again. With literacy, practitioners should avoid sentences like 'That was wrong!' or 'That's not what it says!' but instead should answer incorrect uses with sentences like 'That was great, let's try that again, this time really think about the sound we want to make.'

It's All Connected!

While Cambourne's theory is related to literacy, these elements of learning how to read are interconnected with the other specific areas of learning. For example, children learning mathematics should be immersed in numbers, they should be expected to count forwards and backwards, they should see adults using and utilising numbers to create purpose, and they should be given proper feedback when they use those numbers effectively. As you explore Cambourne's ideas, your task here is to think about how the eight elements connect to the specific areas of learning and how you could use them effectively.

Now let's look at how we could support the early learning goals in the specific areas for EAL children.

Supporting Early Learning Goals

Children with EAL come to us as a non-uniform experience. Some children come to us with a prolonged experience of English, and some come to us with nothing. Both examples may well be found in the same early years setting. The needs of these children will differ vastly and can create a particular challenge for even the most prepared practitioner. How we utilise assessment strategies in the setting is of particular importance.

Areas of the EYFS, with the exception of communication, language, and literacy, can actually be assessed in a child's native language. However it is unlikely that the majority of practitioners will have the capability to assess a child in their native language, and if they can, it's unlikely this assessment will apply to all children given that EAL children are unlikely to come to us with the same native language in every case.

Practitioners who do speak a child's home language should be cautious of over- utilising this as a means to teach. A child living in the UK will need English, and the focus here should be on the target language.

Proper assessment within the key areas of learning comes from a proper understanding of the Early Learning Goals, as per the new Department of Education EYFS framework and below you will find some ideas of how to support the learning goals, and what to look for more specifically as you work to support EAL children in your care.

Supporting Early Learning Goals (Literacy)

Word Reading

Are representations of the child's home language available in the setting?

Are there representation of the alphabet and numbers?

Practitioners can use these as a benchmark for reading to see if children understand their own alphabet before engaging them in the English alphabet. As we assess opportunities for reading development, examples of reading should be everywhere in the setting, and this applies not just to EAL children but to native speakers of English too. This could include:

- Display boards
- Provocations
- Letters and sounds matching
- Synthetic Phonics lessons
- Bilingual books

Inevitably, reading skills must be assessed in English; however, developing the context and concept of reading can be done in the home language too. It is important for practitioners to make parents aware that reading really is a fundamental aspect of learning the English language.

Writing

Can children recognise and write their own names? This is a key indicator for writing, as well as the recognisable development of strong tripod pencil grip. As children develop their writing skills, you should see children give meaning to the marks they make, regardless of whether these marks are representative of actual words. This could pose a particular challenge for practitioners with EAL children because the meaning given might not be incredibly clear. Even if the child is being imaginative, he or she might not know the vocabulary in English. Practitioners can assess this by having visual representation present near writing areas. From here, we can work on the alphabet and into CVC words such as cat, dog, etc.

Writing areas should also be multicultural, with cultural areas having demonstrations of different writing systems, for example Chinese/Japanese calligraphy.

Supporting Early Learning Goals (Literacy)

Number

Arguably the easiest thing for practitioners do to encourage or to assess mathematics skill would be to learn the number system from one to ten in the child's native language and use these in the first few weeks. This initial assessment will allow practitioners to come to an agreed benchmark for numbers and counting. Practitioners should not feel nervous or embarrassed to use a second language that they're not familiar with to speak with a child, and should recognise that when a child hears their home language, they will naturally feel inclined to bond with the practitioner.

From here, practitioners can introduce and use number language related to English and the key skills that children need to learn for the early learning goal, for example introducing addition and subtraction activities during kitchen role-play.

Numerical Patterns

Once a child is building their foundation in numbers and counting, so then can we introduce ways to manipulate numbers. As children are expected to verbally count beyond 20, children should always have access to these number systems in the setting. Consistency is important in both language and mathematical development. To ensure that children are comfortable with numerical patterns practitioners can:

1. Provide visual representations in the setting, particularly the classroom where EAL children are learning.
2. Regularly count, add, and subtract in front of children, ensuring children take part in this practice.
3. Provide shared learning opportunities whereby children will be responsible for providing a certain number of items for other children, thus helping them practise their counting skills on a personal level.

Supporting Early Learning Goals (Understanding the World)

Past and Present

Past and present can be particularly difficult grammatical concepts for an EAL child to understand. While the early learning goal expects children to talk about the lives of people around them and to know similarities and differences between things in the past and things that are happening now, practitioners must have patience with the idea that children will struggle with this concept. To help children understand past and present, practitioners can:

1. Provide visual representations of historical sites then and now.
2. Read stories and introduce narratives that display a clear timeline.
3. Discuss the activities of the week using grammatical terms such as yesterday and last week to show children a changing timeline.
4. Take photos of the environment and show a timeline of the environment evolving so that children understand the difference between past and present.

People and Communities

People and Communities is a very interesting goal to explore with an EAL child because the early learning goal includes learning about diverse cultures and, as we have explored in this book, there are a wide range of cultures for us to explore in our settings. Whether it be European, Asian, American, African, or Australian, these children are likely to have already ingrained into their upbringing a cultural heritage that's different and unique from the UK. To encourage understanding more about people and communities:

1. Encourage children/families to share aspects with us from their cultural heritage; the more of this we see in the setting, the more rich elements of culture children can learn about. This also applies to the British children in your class as the learning experience is expected to be all-encompassing.
2. Encourage children to bring items and things from home that they can share with us.
3. Host cultural festivals/days whereby the setting celebrates different holidays, foods, and traditions.

The Natural World

As children explore the natural world around them, they're expected to make observations of wildlife and plant life and understand differences and similarities between different environments, as well as understanding important processes and changes around them. To explore this for an EAL child, practitioners could:

1. Engage children in creative art and engage their creative sides; nature is often quite vibrant and messy and children should engage with it on this level too.
2. Incorporate technology by considering having children take photos of nature and the natural world; these are great methods to encourage conversation and spoken word.
3. Explore multicultural elements of the entire natural world, not just those things found within in the UK.

Creating with Materials

Practitioners should utilise music wherever possible to help EAL children adapt to creative language in the setting. Music helps children to engage with:

1. Songs and dances
2. Rhymes and rhythms
3. Media materials which help children to discover further literacy and mathematics

Children should also be encouraged to take safe risks with materials in art corners, creating patterns and being given access to representations of culturally diverse art that can be recreated and discussed in circle times.

Being Imaginative and Expressive

Provide all children with opportunities to explore culturally diverse art, music, creative play, free play, and outdoor play. There's no limit to imagination, only the limits that we put on ourselves. In the constructivist approach, we let the children lead the way because what they're thinking should be communicated to us in any way possible and when children, especially EAL children, are given the opportunity to be imaginative they're given the opportunity to communicate to us in ways that we might not expect and this is always a positive thing.

To enhance this creativity, consider:

1. Arranging visits to the setting from a variety of people in the community who can discuss a wide range of topics with the children.
2. Arrange trips to other places where children can experience things they might not have experienced before, even if this is the local library; a library to a child is not just a collection of books but might be a maze in which they can explore.
3. Use your own imagination – think of the things you would enjoy playing with now and try to make them child-centric. Remember, when we enjoy things, the children tend to enjoy them too.

Finally...

Try to have fun! The learning areas and learning goals are meant to excite and inspire, so enjoy yourself and enjoy creating ideas within them!

The reader should now have explored the specific areas in more detail as they relate to the experience of an EAL child. Chapter 5 will further explore how to overcome the most common issues faced by EAL learners.

FURTHER READING TO SUPPORT CHAPTER 4

1. Longstaffe, M. (2020). *Provocations for Learning in the Early Years: A Practical Guide.* London: Jessica Kingsley Publishers.

Overcoming Challenges for EAL Children

In this chapter, we will explore core challenges that practitioners and children alike are likely to face when approaching a curriculum or framework through a second language. We will look at key strategies for overcoming these challenges and strategise on how to work with EAL children to provide the best environment.

Introduction

When any child joins a new school in the UK, they are expected to engage with British culture and British education; however the curriculum/frameworks we use in the UK arguably expect children to come with an existing knowledge of the English language.

We can assume that most children coming to us from British-born families are already developing their language skills in English and for these children, a practitioner will oversee a more typical development. When practitioners work with EAL children, however, we are dealing with atypical development, and this poses its own unique set of challenges.

We often associate the term 'atypical' with SEND children, but please keep in mind as you work with SEND children that EAL is not the same as SEND and the strategies are, and should be, quite different. Practitioners working with EAL children must consider the importance of quality preparation as a tool of education.

Within the dominant early years frameworks (EYFS, Montessori, Reggio Emilia, Te Whariki) the role of planning and preparation is done

DOI: 10.4324/9781003190219-6

collaboratively with children in a constructivist pattern of planning and assessment but when we are planning for EAL children, contingencies must be put in place to ensure we have a quality awareness of the real difficulties EAL children face as they spend time in an early years setting.

Furthermore, it is essential that practitioners are also being mindful of the difficulties they themselves will face when working with children with EAL. And here I would offer a key piece of advice to practitioners; we cannot be everything to everyone and it's OK to have difficulties. What makes a great educator is how we reflect on these difficulties and continue to help those in need.

Re-Defining EAL

I recommend you to now go to the '**Defining EAL**' page in the Introduction to this book and reflect on what you think an EAL child is, or how this term can be more closely defined in a setting.

In my experience, teachers often only associate children as being EAL when they are currently unable to speak English proficiently or with ease, however, this is not always the case.

We've already covered some common misconceptions about EAL children, for example, a British passport holder can be an EAL child but being EAL doesn't necessarily tell us anything about a child's fluency in English. We must be very careful with this label, and we must approach EAL children in the same way we approach all children; their needs should be treated as unique.

The EYFS Communication and Language framework is designed for those children whose first language is English; however, practitioners should reflect on the fact that the developmental stages within the framework are not specific to English, they are specific to language. Let's look at the following example from the *What to Expect, When?* (2015) document:

30 to 50 months you might notice that...

Speaking

I am beginning to use longer sentences with words like 'because' and 'and' like 'I cried, I did, because I banged my foot'

TIME TO THINK:

If a child is not demonstrating this specific goal in English, but is demonstrating capabilities with this language in their native language would you consider this child to have a language delay?

Reflect on this question with other practitioners.

TIME TO REFLECT:

How could you learn if a child is able to meet this criterion in their home language?

The EAL Group

EAL children will have individual language learning needs as they are a part of a diverse population in a setting. As with all learners, the EAL group must be seen as a unique group. Practitioners must always keep in mind that EAL learners face multiple challenges in their learning:

- They have to acquire both academic and colloquial English.
- They must develop within a framework delivered in English.
- They must overcome the culturally-bound aspect of schooling.

(Franson, 2008)

Furthermore, there are specific areas of challenge that practitioners need to anticipate in order to plan for.

Cultural/Social Challenges

As we are currently exploring the support we can offer to children from culturally diverse backgrounds, it is also important for practitioners to be aware of how their perception of other cultures could affect their practice. 'Stereotyping' is a very sensitive topic nowadays, but research does show that there is still a practice of stereotyping children based on their ethnic background. As an example, there is a belief that children from Indian, Japanese, Chinese, Korean, and Polish backgrounds are perceived as the 'model minorities', coming from a background considered to be high achieving (Ng, Lee, and Pak, 2007). This kind of stereotyping can lead to a variety of problems, especially if the child in question does not fall in line with a pre-existing notion of their abilities.

This stereotyping works two ways, and conversely, research also shows that certain ethnic minority groups do not receive a positive label but rather are perceived as underperforming, which in turn leads to a lower teacher expectation (Gillborn and Mirza, 2000).

Furthermore, children will come to your setting with pre-existing notions of discipline and adult-child interaction. These are likely to differ with your approach and may lead to a child experiencing a period of misunderstanding as you both navigate this cultural exchange.

Children who are new to the setting are also likely to experience feelings of isolation, particularly if they left their home country before attending any form of formal education. Similarly, if a child has experienced schooling that is interrupted, they are likely to feel overwhelmed. Children new to English will also experience difficulty in communicating their base needs, exacerbating any feelings of isolation.

The setting routines will offer a new landscape of exploration for children; however,those new to English may miss out on these opportunities if they are not provided with explicit instruction on how to access this landscape (Cameron, Moon, and Bygate 1996).

Critical Reflection

Are you guilty of cultural stereotyping?

If you are, then good news for you, it's not too late to change!

Language/Learning Challenges

When children come to us from other countries, we must take into consideration the education background a child may have experienced. The EYFS is a largely child-driven vehicle, but the same cannot be said for kindergartens and nurseries around the world.

Take, for example, the local system of Hong Kong, where children as young as 3 are taught in a didactic classroom to read, write, and recognise hundreds of Chinese characters. The local system expects children to sit, listen, and learn and often when these children transition into a play-based approach, they experience a period of confusion when they're able to direct their own learning.

As children transition into your setting, you may notice that activities that require open-ended problem solving pose an issue when a child is used to close-ended work. In addition to this, any learning will take place in English, and this further distances the child from the learning environment.

As we've discussed, EAL is not in the same category as SEND, yet in some settings, these two branches are considered the same. As planning for SEND children is hyper-specific to their additional needs, this type of planning cannot be utilised for EAL children without restricting their time engaging in English.

And finally, take into account the difficulties children can face when they are using reading and writing systems that differ from those used in their native languages. Languages that are alphabetic can have vastly different pronunciations depending on the child's first language, and languages that are logographic (like Chinese and Japanese) are far removed from the written language a child will see in the setting.

Staffing

Children who come to an early years setting with English as an additional language face the task of learning language within the context of a mainstream curriculum. The support and collaboration we put in place between adults at the school is imperative to the successes that children will have during their EAL provision. Settings should consider how to utilise staff effectively in order to have a structured support system in place for children, families, and teachers of EAL. In terms of structure, settings may choose to employ any number of the following staff members to assist EAL families and children. The following list is adapted from South (2012):

- EAL Consultants
- EAL Coordinators
- Specialist Teachers
- Bilingual Teaching Assistants
- One-to-one Support Workers

If a setting is fortunate enough to have any number of these staff, they will be given a greater ability to work together to support practitioners of the early years within the setting environment. Unfortunately, staffing in the early years is a difficult topic to approach, now more than ever, and it is apparent that in many settings there are few EAL specialists; rather, other staff take a role in EAL teaching. Without proper support and guidance, it's hard to determine if staff involved in EAL teaching are providing the right support in settings. As far as what settings could do, having staff take on any of the following responsibilities provides the setting with an atmosphere of responsibility for children who are EAL.

EAL Consultants

Consultants generally work on whole-school development and mainstream teacher professional development rather than offering specialist teaching support for learners in the setting. Consultant roles were once strengthened by national strategy initiatives in order to address the needs of EAL and ethnic minority learners; however, with funding being a constant issue in the UK education system, the number of consultants has decreased significantly.

EAL Coordinators

Coordinators are likely to be on-site specialist teachers who have a prime responsibility for EAL learners or who manage a team of bilingual and specialist teaching assistants and other support staff. In some schools, this role is adopted by the SEN coordinator; however, arguments could be made against having the same person responsible for SEN and EAL. As we've discussed, EAL and SEN are not the same thing and must be approached on different spectrums of support. On the EAL side of the spectrum, responsibilities might include:

- Advising on resourcing for EAL children
- Developing CPD for staff
- Supporting colleagues to develop their knowledge of how being EAL affects children's lives
- Action planning school improvement
- Planning and teaching
- Developing practice to meet the needs of language learners and their families

Specialist Teachers

Specialist teachers in a setting should work with different early years groups, supporting teachers by utilising their understanding of second language learning in young children. A specialist teacher should take into account the purposes for which children need to use English and should produce strategies for both whole class and individual child development. The specialist teacher should act as a resource for EAL children and recognise the need for pupils to learn curriculum content through a second language.

Bilingual Teaching Assistant

Martin-Jones and Saxena (2003) investigated the role of bilingual teaching assistants in schools and found that bilingual teaching assistants acted not only as a bilingual resource for teachers in working with pupils but also as providers of valuable support for learners, making links between home and school-based contexts for learning. A bilingual teaching assistant might be the perfect person to form an attachment or an initial bond when a child joins a setting, especially if there is a shared language and cultural heritage with the pupils coming to the setting. A bilingual teaching assistant activates the prior cultural and language knowledge of a child with EAL. Settings will likely run into difficulties when selecting a bilingual teaching assistant, as schools do not have infinite resources but may have multiple languages spoken in the setting. How schools utilise bilingual teaching assistants is largely up to them; however, this is one area where early years settings should be forward-thinking.

As settings develop their staffing needs, so too can they better put strategies in place to support EAL children.

Teaching and Learning

As practitioners, we play a critical role in ensuring that children have access to, and engage in, play experiences during the learning process. Practitioners of the early years are often overlooked in the world of education. Why is this? Mainly because early years is not seen to be as important as other areas of education. I find this to be a falsehood, but often many have a perception that early years practitioners simply must just be 'good with kids' and this is seen as sufficient. But early years education is not babysitting. It is at times a hard and difficult process that requires technical knowledge, specialist support, and above all, patience.

But these skills alone are not sufficient and organising learning experiences such as a home corners and phonics displays only take us so far in the learning process. What is most important is how a practitioner engages with children and their play.

When practitioners work with EAL children, we must consider how our guidance must be tailored to meet the needs of this specific child in conjunction with supporting language learning. In order for our interactions with play to have the best effect, an EAL child's play journey requires a heightened level of support through teacher interaction. Practitioners need to keep in mind the importance of:

* Observation
* Participation
* Assessment/Reflection
* Planning

Meeting successes with EAL children means observing not only their behaviour, but also their interests, and will aim to see the world as the child sees it. Being a play partner means entering an activity through the gaze of the child's own imagination and exploring in the same way that they do. As a participant to this activity, practitioners should be respectful of the will of the child and aim to guide the child further in the activity, paying special attention to the language being used.

Through Play

There is a reason that we place play opportunities at the pinnacle of our education practices in the early years and this is because play creates more meaningful contexts for children. These contexts (which are key!) are learning gold for an EAL child, who will be given opportunities to communicate in both verbal and non-verbal ways. Children are provided with comfortable periods in which they can practice familiar words and begin the process of hearing and combining entirely new language together.

A practitioner can utilise a number of key language development practices here, such as:

- creative commentary
- naming and labelling
- asking questions
- rehearsing sentence structures
- modelling useful language

A child who is not able to talk for themselves requires practitioners to be sensitive to the needs of the child and furthermore, practitioners should take opportunities in play to extend children's response. As we observe children at play, we can initiate and incorporate more complex sentences and sentence structures that children can then use.

Critical Questions

How much talking is too much?
When does an interaction become an interference?

Teacher Interaction

'Shared, sustained thinking' (Sylva et al., 2004) is identified as an important aspect of adult-child interaction. This means that the quality of the interactions, and the time during which an activity is sustained, is an important aspect for practitioners be aware of within the teaching and learning environment.

Sylva et al. (2004) researched the quality of adult–child interactions and discovered that high quality interactions (shared, sustained thinking) was the leading characteristic that separated successful teachers from struggling teachers.

How this applies to EAL children is of particular importance as an EAL child is likely to have a lower amount of interaction with other children and with adults. This in turn could add to the confusion a child feels with the learning environment.

Current research unfortunately suggests that many practitioners of the early years actually distance themselves from their bilingual children (Drury, 2007) and this could be due to any number of reasons. As we've explored how staffing can help to avoid these issues, it might be prudent to approach leadership in settings and inquire as to how staff could be put in place to better support EAL children.

Playing with Others

Play is often distinguished as a very changing experience. Children's exploration can be sporadic and because of this, opportune moments to engage with a child can be missed. My advice here is not to count the failures but focus more heavily on every moment you do catch. Practitioners will need to find a strong balance in the moments they engage with, because whilst there are some moments that may be missed, equally there may be moments where a practitioner's involvement is not required. Ask yourself:

1. Is my involvement directly changing the plan a child may have had?
2. Is my involvement preventing a child from engaging with their peers?
3. Is my involvement beneficial to the child?
4. During our interaction is the child in control of their play?

No practitioner will ever get this 100% right, but generally a practitioner should make themselves available to play, and available to observe, joining in only when it seems appropriate and positively influential on the learning environment. For an EAL child, language learning is dependent on social interaction with multiple parties, not just with key adults. How are you as a practitioner facilitating interactions with peers? Keep this question in your mind when deciding whether to interact during play and reflect on your behaviour as it pertains to peer interaction. This is of vital importance in the early years because a child's interest is likely to be further sustained when he or she is playing with peers. Playing with peers provides opportunity for meaningful communication, opportunities for creative language development, social skill development, negotiation skill development, and these are optimal language learning opportunities.

There is a key difference between adults to child interactions and child to child interactions in that when children play together, they often do so as equals. Children will work to create a joint agreement on the purpose of their interaction and can be seen encouraging and supporting each other as they engage in imaginative play. An observant practitioner might notice here language being used that is coming from other parts of the setting. As an example, children may rehearse their own rules that are reflective of the rules of practitioners put in place during circle time. Children might be heard saying things like 'two minutes till we tidy up', and this shows a key understanding of the context of language. As we have discussed, EAL children require a certain level of consistency and when they engage in play with their peers, they are given access to this consistency.

Practitioners of the early years should always incorporate rich language uses in their daily routine and should always provide opportunities for children to play with each other throughout the day.

Timeline of EAL Development

Studies have provided us with recognisable stages for additional language development and there are benefits to recognising different stages of language development:

1. They provide an additional framework for the practitioner to use.
2. They provide benchmarks for progress.
3. They provide language specific learning opportunities.

Second language development, like all areas of the early years, can generally be considered as a stages not ages approach, so practitioners should take care when looking at stages of language development, thinking of them more as a guideline as opposed to a set of rules. The stages here are adapted from the work of Clarke (1992) and Tabors (1997) and are generally accepted to be:

1. Continued Use of Home Language

An EAL Child is likely to use their home language for a brief time in the setting to communicate with staff and with peers. When the child realises that their home language can no longer be used, they will enter a silent stage.

2. The Silent Stage

In almost every case, practitioners will likely see the silent stage, and this stage will be observed shortly after a child joins the setting and could last anywhere up to six months. Children require an adequate adjustment to acclimate to the new language they are surrounded by. Further to this, a child is simultaneously learning what is expected of them in the setting. As this acclimatisation takes place, children are also likely to engage in practice and rehearsal of the language they're hearing around them.

Clarke (1992) put forward 10 key strategies to support children during the silent stage:

1. Continued talking even when children do not respond
2. Persistent inclusion in small groups with other children
3. Use of varied questions
4. Inclusion of other children as the focus in the conversation
5. Use of the first language

6. Acceptance of non-verbal responses
7. Praising of minimal effort
8. Expectations to respond with repeated words and/or counting
9. Structuring of programme to encourage child to child interaction
10. Provide activities which reinforce language practice through role play

3. Repetition and Play, Use of Formulae, Routines, and Single Words

Practitioners should observe children gaining confidence in the English language, but this may start with individual words and phrases. You may note here the children are using holophrases regularly. A holophrase is a word used that represents an entire language structure. For example, a child looks at you and says the word 'water'; this could be considered a holophrase. Our role as practitioners is to understand what the meaning of this holophrase is. It could be any of the following:

- I'm thirsty and I want some water!
- Can I play in the water?
- It's raining outside.
- I spilled my water and I need help.

Once a practitioner has discovered this meaning, they should echo the child's language and have a child repeat using more complex language structures. From here a practitioner should notice the child beginning to develop productive use of English as an additional language (Tabors, 1997).

Language uses at this time may also include familiar language used on a daily basis, such as language associated with routine, clean up time, or familiar songs and rhymes.

4. More Complex English or Productive Language Use

This is the stage at which an EAL child demonstrates productive uses of the additional language. The child should be extending on their existing knowledge and showing evidence of understanding grammatical structures and how they apply to spoken language. Sentences are likely to become longer and more complex, and a practitioner will know that this stage is taking place because the intent of the language will be very clear.

Don't Overthink!

As we discussed, these stages are not guaranteed 100%. Children will develop through these stages at a rate specific to them and practitioners may see examples of overlapping, regression, or non-compliance with these stages overall. What we want to observe as practitioners is a gradual and slow development. Practitioners should primarily hope to see evidence that children are engaging in more peer-to-peer interactions.

Critical Reflection

EAL children are likely to engage in code-switching and this is perfectly normal. Code-switching is the phenomenon when a child uses two languages in the same sentence, essentially filling the gaps in English with the mother tongue. Research into code-switching suggests that it is a highly intelligent form of language use because children will still adhere to the grammatical rules of the second language while speaking in the first. Code-switching is an indication that the child is learning language appropriately so do expect to see this and celebrate it in the setting.

Top Tips for Supporting EAL Children

Encourage the native language (L1) – Strong development in L1 skills can only be seen as a positive in terms of further development of both language and literacy development in English. Practitioners should encourage parents to talk and read to their children in their home language as a way of strengthening their child's second language. Practitioners should also incorporate a child's home language in the setting where possible. Songs and videos can be used effectively for this purpose if teachers don't speak a child's home language (Gillanders, 2007).

Scaffold with space and routine – The setting should be arranged in such a way that children are supported through instructional activities. While EAL children are becoming confident with their routine, it is important that changes to the physical space are gradual. As children develop confidence and comfort with the physical space, they are likely to use the environment to cue their behaviour in that area (Barone and Xu 2008).

Exposure levels – Children with EAL must be exposed to rich language on a continuous level, and both shared book reading and extended talk time with a practitioner have been shown to enhance a child's expressive language development (Aukrust, 2007). Practitioners could try *creative commentary*. This is the process by which a practitioner provides a running commentary of what's happening in the setting so that children are consistently exposed to language. Creative commentary can be very simple, with practitioners simply vocalising their actions as they take place. This can be enhanced by asking follow-up questions to the child to encourage co-regulation.

Explicit, concise, and systematic instruction – Children with EAL should be exposed to language in an accessible way. Instruction should be given explicitly and concisely, meaning that practitioners should be very clear in what they expect. Practitioners may want to use simple sentences or just key vocabulary to communicate at first, slowly developing this into more complex examples of language as children grow in ability. Instruction should also be systematic, which means it should be done in accordance with a fixed plan that children can become familiar with.

Finally...

Just talk with the children in your care; it's the easiest method of engagement and will bear results when the practitioner keeps trying!

The reader should now have a broader level of understanding of how to support EAL children as they develop within the early years through a second language. Chapter 6 will explore how we can achieve more through the tool of culturally responsive pedagogy.

FURTHER READING TO SUPPORT CHAPTER 5

1. Harries, J. (2016). *The Little Book of Talk.* London: Featherstone.

6 Culturally Responsive Pedagogy

In this chapter, we will explore how culture and pedagogy go hand in hand, and further explore the responsibility that practitioners have in understanding how to incorporate culture into the daily routine of the early years setting.

Introduction

Culturally responsive pedagogy is a more recent phenomenon that is comparative in its nature to the growing demands of Science, Technology, Engineering, Art, and Mathematics, or 'STEAM' education in schools, and because of this, research into culturally responsive pedagogy is still being undertaken. For the early years practitioner, this means that defining and utilising this aspect of education might not be the easiest task. However, culturally responsive pedagogy being a newer phenomenon is also a strength for the budding practitioner, as the field is open to experimentation and exploration.

Our role in education is to always be studying and to always try to explore new ideas as they become part of our work; it's the responsibility of the early years educator to do as we say to the children; we must explore.

If you struggle to incorporate culturally responsive pedagogy into your work, then rest assured that you are not alone! My answer to this struggle is the same answer I give to families when I too am asked a difficult question; *we need to unpack the term.* As we explore this idea in greater detail, using a touch of our holistic approach to understand how it's connected to early

DOI: 10.4324/9781003190219-7

years, we can better understand how cultural responsivity and our pedagogy works together to create a culturally diverse classroom.

Why is it Necessary?

Given the increasing expansion of multicultural dimensions in schools in
the UK, it can and should be (in my opinion) interpreted as a positive phenomenon that our theories of education are moving towards advocating
pedagogy that supports and enhances a supportive learning environment
for children who come from a variety of ethnicities, races, beliefs, religions,
and home backgrounds.

It's important at this time to note that that whilst the focus of this chapter
is of course on supporting the wellbeing of children who come from EAL
backgrounds, the term culture doesn't just apply to families who come from
international backgrounds.

The UK is host to many cultures and these should be celebrated in your
setting regardless of the level at which we experience a cultural difference.
Sometimes families move from the Northern England to the South, and even
though the move is geographically in the same country, this too can be a
culture shock. Some families have different makel-up than others; for example, some children are raised by same-sex parents, raised by grandparents,
raised by foster parents, or are adopted children. These are all examples of
cultural differences that are atypical compared to what we generally see
as the typical norm in British society. I for one think that having culturally
responsive pedagogy challenges the belief that the nuclear family make-up
is the right family makeup, and I believe this is an incredibly positive thing.
No one should dictate how we make a family, but practitioners should try to
be responsive to the experiences of the children in the setting; this is one of
our main responsibilities.

What is Culture?

Being responsive to culture means first having an understanding of the cultural boundaries we are dealing with. We've touched upon culture a little bit

in previous chapters, but let's explore culture in depth so that we can better understand how we can be responsive to it.

TIME TO THINK:

On a piece of paper write down all the things you associate with your cultural heritage. What matters in this task is that you identify the things you write down as important to your culture.

TIME TO REFLECT:

- If you're in a group, share these ideas together see if there are any similarities between you and a colleague.
- If you're alone, think about the history of these things and how they've had an effect on your life so far.
- Reflect on why you think these things are associated to culture.

Exploring Culture

Culture can be a difficult idea to define because of the expansive nature of what can be included in the term. Realistically, there is no one type of culture, and it can mean different things to different people, just like languages.

Take for instance, the reputation of the UK for having a 'drinking culture'. We, as British people, are known for enjoying a good few drinks. On the other end of the spectrum think next of 'sitting Shiva', the week-long Jewish ceremony for mourning the dead. This ceremony is deeply ingrained into the culture and religion of the Jewish people and dictates the expected behaviour during mourning times. These two cultural elements, vastly different from each other with no correlations in their significance, are however both deeply important to the people who identify with these cultures.

This example is not random; it's the first step in understanding the difference between *surface culture* and *deep culture*. Once we understand how culture can be categorised, the difference in culture's significance, and how to explore deep culture further, we can only then begin to understand how to have culturally responsive pedagogy.

Arguably one of the most influential names in the study of culture, Gary Weaver (2000), introduced to us an easy-to-use model of culture that I think practitioners can utilise to better understand the invisible forces working away between people in a multicultural setting.

Surface Culture

Weaver (2000) asks us to imagine culture as an iceberg. When you see the iceberg bobbing up and down in the water, what you see is only 10 per cent of the whole structure – the rest is hidden underwater. The top of the iceberg represents the surface culture, in the same way that what we often see in other cultures is about 10 per cent of the actual culture. Surface culture can be defined using 5 'F' words; fortunately they're probably not the 'F' words you're thinking of. They are:

1. Food
2. Flags
3. Festivals
4. Fashion
5. Famous people

Critical Reflection

Do any of the things in your previous list related to your own culture fall under the banner of the 5 Fs?

LEARNING EXAMPLE

Kanon is a preschool student in a small preschool. Kanon is origi-
nally from Japan and both of her parents speak moderate English.
In an attempt to make Kanon feel more comfortable in the setting,
the practitioners created a culture wall exploring Japanese culture.
They added some Japanese katakana (alphabet for representing
English words, i.e. コンピューター, *konpyuta – computer), some*
pictures of sushi, a Japanese flag, a box containing Japanese num-
bers, and some other things depicting kawaii (cute) culture.

TIME TO REFLECT:

* Analyse the contents of the display for yourself.
* What is your overall assessment of the display?

Analysis

You could rationalise that the display is a good start, at the very least acknowledging some cultural differences in the student body. However, what we learn from the display about the child, or about Japan, is very little. Many of the things in the display could be described as tropes; oversimpli-fied ideas of what a culture could be. The display doesn't give us an indica-tion of how to work with the Japanese family or how to engage in Japanese language, it doesn't tell me what social norms a Japanese family follows, or how to interact with them, and other than acting as a tokenistic discussion topic once or twice with a family, the display doesn't really give us many opportunities to extend parent partnership either.

What we need to know as practitioners are all the things that make up our interaction with the family and our interactions with the child. As we explore the other 90 per cent, the rest of the iceberg that we can't see, we will begin to understand why deep culture is so significant in our lives as educators.

TIME TO THINK:

Before reading on, make a list of things you think might be associated with deep culture. Then, look at the list below and see if you can recognise any of your ideas on there. Do any of the included items surprise you?

Deep Culture

Weaver (2000) defines deep culture as all of the cultural elements present in another culture that can't be tangibly seen. These are:

Communication Styles & Rules (facial expressions, gestures, eye contact, personal space, and touching)
Notions (courtesy and manners, friendship, leadership, modesty, and expressing emotions)
Concepts (self, time, past and future, and the roles taken according to age, sex, class, family)
Attitudes (elders, adolescents, dependents, rules, expectations, work)
Approaches (religion, raising children, making decisions, problem solving)

The work of Gary Weaver has opened our eyes to the expansive nature of culture and its effects on our ability to engage in the classroom.

Critical Reflection

Have you noticed any of the elements of deep culture in your interactions with EAL families?

Only as we explore these aspects of culture and begin to familiarise ourselves with the importance of deep culture can we start to work on cultural competency.

Cultural Competency

Cultural competency defines our ability to work alongside, teach, and interact with people from different cultures. As we develop this competency, so too will our pedagogy become responsive to cultural differences.

In order to develop this competency, practitioners should be aware of:

1. Their own culture, and how it plays a part in their own lives. Understanding parts of ourselves is often an important step in understanding others.
2. How willing they are to engage and participate in both the surface and deep elements of another culture.
3. How their attitude towards people of other cultures is perceived, positively or negatively.

Practitioners should regularly be reflecting on these questions and should be actively discovering how cultural competency develops and grows over the course of time spent in a setting.

Cultural Learners

Children in an early years setting are undertaking a monumental task; their formative years are pivotal to their development, and professionals in the early years must be able to meet the diverse cultural and language needs of children in their care. Only through this ability to meet needs can children be exposed to the quintessential learning and development needed.

Think back to our exploration of the holistic approach in previous chapters, and consider how it's important now more than ever to think holistically as we explore the variety of elements that affect an EAL child's experience in the early years.

The little ones in our care are also developing their own cultural competency and keep this in mind as you're teaching. As multicultural learners, be aware of the following:

- Regardless of what language children speak they're still developing and learning.
- Children who were raised in languages other than English still have previously acquired knowledge.
- Children have learned how to make relationships in their home language.
- Home language is tied to culture (Chang, 1993).
- Practitioners should respect children's cultural backgrounds.

Your Background

As we recognise that children are born belonging to a culture that predates their parents and may involve traditional practices, values, and knowledge, we also must recognise that culture is informed by experiences in the family as individuals and as part of various other communities.

There is a sense of belonging that each child will experience within their cultural community and it is the role of the early years educator to offer a similar sense of belonging by helping children to build on their existing abilities that may have come from their cultural dimensions and help children to achieve their educational potential.

Being culturally competent does not just mean being accepting of other cultures. There's sometimes a misconception in Western countries that making space for another culture means taking space from the existing culture, foregoing our own cultural experiences in order to make other cultures feel comfortable. This, however, is the opposite of cultural competency as the whole idea behind cultural competency is understanding our background, understanding the background of someone else, and understanding how they can work together. You already have a great list above of how to explore people's deep culture but let's think a little bit of hard to develop your own cultural competency.

Think about the following things:

- What have your experiences been like in life so far?
- What are your main values?
- What would you name as your community?
- What's your key knowledge of your own family and community history?
- Have you ever been faced with cultural differences because of your culture?
- How do your memories of your culture as a child compare with your memories of today?

Critical Reflection

How do your answers to these questions match or differ from those of your colleagues?

Starting the Conversation

It's time to put our knowledge into practice and this often starts with having a conversation. It is important for settings to encourage open communication in regards to culture, cultural difference, and cultural competency. Formal instruction in early years is becoming more and more open to culturally responsive instruction, and so it stands to reason that the setting should be doing the same. Only in this way can we better support practitioners to advocate for a shift toward pedagogy that is enriching for all children.

The Three Functional Dimensions

Culturally responsive pedagogy is divided into three functional dimensions: the institutional dimension, the personal dimension, and the instructional dimension (Lynch, 2016).

Institutional Dimension – concerns itself with the cultural factors that affect school organisation including school policies and procedures. Within the institutional dimension we can also think about community involvement. Essentially, the institutional dimension looks at culturally responsive pedagogy and the role the entire institution plays in that pedagogy. Ask yourself the following questions to see if your institution is engaging well in culturally responsive pedagogy:

1. Do we have policies and procedures in place that protect cultural, religious, and ethnic freedoms?
2. What training have we had to help us work better with culturally diverse children?
3. As an institution, are we a positive force in the community?
4. Are there strategies in place that ensure a diverse host of children and families can access our institution?

Personal Dimension – concerns itself with the continuous development of teachers in the area of culturally responsive pedagogy. As we've explored in this chapter, there are things we can do to understand culture, but how are we acting upon what we know and what evidence are we showing in the classrooms that our practice is culturally responsive. Ask yourself these questions:

1. What do I know about the cultural background of each of my children?
2. Can I provide evidence of how I have identified the strengths of my culturally diverse children?
3. How does my planning reflect cultural responsivity in the setting?

Instructional Dimension – concerns itself with the more practical element of creating an environment that has cultural responsiveness as part of its pedagogy.

1. How am I celebrating the cultural background of each of my children?
2. How does my planning reflect cultural responsivity in the setting?
3. How am I evolving my environment to reflect culturally responsive pedagogy?

A truly rich, holistic, and culturally responsive environment has the power to shape and develop key skills for young children like self-regulation, divergent thinking, and executive function. Moreover, culturally responsive pedagogy prepares all of our children for a globalised society.

Tips to Practice Culturally Responsive Pedagogy

Think About Inclusion

Reflect on your planning and teaching practice and consider how this relates to or applies to all the children in your class. As an example, when using stories or festivals in your teaching practice, consider the diverse festivals that children in your class will take part in. Chinese New Year is just as important as Christmas to some families and including this is an important part of culturally responsive pedagogy. Having children work together in diverse groups to explore festivals creates a rich learning environment for all children. As children become confident in the setting, so too will they begin to develop positive memories and learning experiences from the class. By offering a variety of culturally responsive opportunities in the classroom, children are given the chance to show off their own values, knowledge, and experiences, which truly creates a welcoming environment for the EAL child.

Think About Depth

Connect the classroom and learning environment to the real world. Incorporate the opinions and ideas of real children into planning and into the classroom environment. For an EAL child this is particularly useful because they're developing their language skills along with their knowledge of the world. How we incorporate this into our planning is up to us but as an example you might incorporate different recipes and discuss with children what foods they like and what foods they dislike, always pushing them to explain why, and helping them to organise their thoughts into how food is representative of culture. As we explore these ideas with children and show that we value their contributions, we are using depth to foster confidence from our children. Confidence goes hand in hand with good quality learning and with the development of English language skills.

Think About People

First and foremost, learn about your children using some of the methods we've discussed in this book. The more information you have about a child and their home life the easier you will find incorporating culturally responsive pedagogy into the classroom. Open communication with children is not just vital for building a bond but also developing English language skills. From here think about guest speakers you could bring in to enrich the learning environment. Grandparents and parents are the easiest guests to ask to come in, but a setting might also utilise diverse members of the local community to come in and talk about their culture their background language. Even something as simple as a cooking display from a local chef who specialises in diverse cuisines would bring an amazing culturally responsive approach to the classroom, especially if the guest speaker is reflective of the type of children you have in your class.

Think About Representations

The children in your class are more likely to process the learning environment when their culture language and background has a place in the setting. This can be easily incorporated almost immediately by thinking about the media you use in the classroom. Ensure that books, art, videos, and photographs all represent a range of different cultures and backgrounds and have these be reflective of what you're doing in your planning. As children recognise multicultural media and how it applies to their day, so too are they more likely to engage in their own form of culturally responsive practice.

Finally...

Have fun! Exploring culture is a gift and allows for us to expand our own thinking as well as expand those things we can enjoy.

The reader should now have a broader idea of culture and the role it plays in our classroom environment. Chapter 7 will help us to explore one of the most important aspects of a child's life – their home life!

FURTHER READING TO SUPPORT CHAPTER 6

1. Borkett, P. (2018). *Cultural Diversity and Inclusion in Early Years Education*. London: Routledge.

Engaging EAL Families

In this chapter, we will explore key methods of interacting with and engaging families from diverse backgrounds, notably those who come to us with English as an Additional Language.

Introduction

Engaging families of other backgrounds starts with introspection. We must first look to ourselves, our own feelings, and relation to culture before we can begin to extend the invitation to other cultures and before we can explore typical parent partnership we have to keep in mind that when caring for children of EAL backgrounds, their parents are also likely to be EAL. Working alongside those who use English as a second language requires some consideration for cultural difference too.

We explored in Chapter 1 the importance that language has in relation to culture, and we explored in Chapter 6 the importance of culturally responsive pedagogy. We must reflect on these two key issues before any form of support can take place for an EAL family. Practitioners must spend some time learning about the cultural history of the family they are working with.

Cultural Dimensions

Cultural dimensions are commonly used to understand and interpret other cultures, but what is a cultural dimension? What does that word mean to you? When we think of cultural dimensions, we could be thinking of any of the following:

DOI: 10.4324/9781003190219-8

- Personal values
- Religious belief
- Social background
- Ethnicity
- Ancestry
- Home environment
- Home language

As we've explored the topic of avoiding placing minority children into categories, practitioners must also avoid making surface level assumptions about other cultures and must try to more closely understand how a personal culture can have an effect on a family in your setting.

One of the easiest ways to do this is to simply ask! To demonstrate this point, I'll ask you in this chapter to explore your own culture in greater depth. During this process you might learn a little bit more about yourself, but you also might further develop a comfort level with the prospect of *exploring culture* generally. You may already be at this point; however, one of the key issues we face in education is the worry that we will *offend* those from a different culture by enquiring.

I've always found asking about cultures, showing an interest in other cultures, and learning about other people's cultures to be an incredibly positive thing. The questions below can help you on the journey of discovery.

Please consider that not everyone is comfortable sharing all of the information in the questions below and they should be respected if this activity is done in a group.

TIME TO THINK:

Fill out the following questionnaire as a group and compare answers together. You may be surprised that people who we assume would be in the same cultural dimensions as ourselves are not:

- Where and when were you born?
- Where did you grow up?
- Where did your parents and grandparents grow up?

- What is your earliest memory as a family?
- What types of important issues did you discuss with your family?
- When major decisions are made in your family, who participates?
- As a family, what events did you celebrate?
- As an adult, what events or holidays do you still celebrate?
- What foods consisted of the family meal?
- What languages do you speak?
- How do you greet people you don't know?
- What is a comfortable physical talking distance between you and a colleague?
- How do you view being tactile with friends or colleagues?
- When timekeeping, do you view time as linear or fluid?
- Do you discuss your faults, feelings, and problems with people outside of your family?
- Do you prefer getting information in words or with a diagram?
- When learning a new skill, do you prefer one step at a time or all information at once?
- Do you believe that individuals are in control of their own destiny or that everything happens for a reason?
- What racial, ethnic, socioeconomic, and religious groups do you identify with?
- What is your earliest memory of belonging to a group other than your family?
- What is your earliest memory of being excluded from a group?
- What is your earliest memory of excluding someone else from a group?

(Adapted from Wintz, S. and Cooper, E., 2000–2003)

TIME TO REFLECT:

Spend some time with your colleagues discussing the answers to the above questions; look for similarities and differences between yourself and them. There are no right or wrong answers when it comes to cultural dimensions. We're most likely to view cultural dimensions occurring between people of different countries, but cultural difference as we see it now can be across ages (Baby Boomers, Millennials, Gen Z), across cities and towns, across social classes, and can even be recognised across accents and dialects.

With that in mind, let's pause our EAL stream and contextualise cultural difficulties into the dominant language of this book, English. Within the English language we can find multiple dialects, and a dialect quite simply is the form of a language which is specific to a region or social group.

Dialects are the reason that someone living near Inverness would boast of their famous *loch* (lake) when someone in Liverpool would talk about their day of shopping in the *chocker* (busy) town centre.

When we're able to look at our own language and examine how it's affected by our own culture, we can begin to scratch the surface of the difficulties that EAL families have when trying to adjust to the environment in the United Kingdom.

In the same way that you may by now know a little bit more about your colleagues, we can also hope to know more about our families by asking questions and learning about their background.

Parent Partnership

So now it's time to apply the same logic to the parents in our schools. It's unlikely that we would ever give parents a questionnaire of this nature, because it could be bordering on inappropriate to expect an EAL family to provide this level of information. However, it could be considered best practice to include a series of questions about home culture in a parent interview before their child joins the school.

How can we define parent partnership?

Parent partnership falls on a spectrum, and we can explore this a little bit more together but first let's have a look at the following case study.

LEARNING EXAMPLE

Andrew is the parent of a four-year-old boy. When he signed his child up to an early years setting, part of the application form asked parents how they would like to get involved in school culture. Andrew ticks several boxes. He agrees to do some maintenance work for the nursery should they need it, he agrees to attend parent evenings and parent conferences, and he offers to also be part of a family group via social media. During the course of the first six months, Andrew is asked to fix a fence panel in the outdoor area on one occasion. He never engages with the school in any other way apart from the yearly parents' evening at the end of the year.

TIME TO THINK:

Is this level of parent engagement enough?

Could the school have provided more opportunities for parent partnership?

TIME TO REFLECT:

When we think about parent partnership, we can plan a number of activities to encourage parents to engage with the early years setting; however, many schools would prefer that parents were not involved in anything of substance. This doesn't mean that schools don't value parent partnership, but schools often want the educational side of a setting left to the educators.

> What are your thoughts on this approach?
> Can you think of three examples where parents could be actively
> engaged in the educational aspect of a school?

Exceeding Activities

Parent partnership exceeds simply asking parents to be a part of activities in the school. Parent partnership is about making parents feel that they are making a positive impact on school culture. How we do this can be affected by school policy, and teacher and family preference. Some families are content with the basic interactions, and this is okay. When we work with families, we must gauge their response and need from parent partnership.

Engaging EAL Families

An EAL family may exhibit some reluctance to partner with a setting in any real way, and the first consideration for practitioners is to determine whether this reluctance is due to disinterest, or due to fear of embarrassment. EAL families are viewing cultural dimensions in the same way that a practitioner is, only from the opposite end of the spectrum.

Statistics Time

Studies by the Greater London Authority (2020) found that as of 2017, even when adjusted for undercounting, there are an estimated 10,320,000 foreign-born residents in the UK. Of this, an estimated 10 per cent are children and young people being raised in environments where English is not the dominant language at home. Legal immigration statistics alone show the continued growth of globalisation happening in the UK.

This statistic shows the sheer number of families that early years settings are working with across the country, and for this reason, practitioners should be regularly thinking about how to support EAL families.

Sharing Cultures

From my own experience in different cultures, I have found various cultures guilty of only one thing: they're all excited to share their experiences, their language, their food, and their culture with people foreign to their home. This is one of the first key ways we can begin to support parent partners in early years settings in the United Kingdom. This approach can be done in three steps:

Step One: Ask Informal Questions

These can be non-invasive yet inviting questions for families to share more about themselves when they're on a school tour. While the objective of a show-round is for parents to learn about the setting, a secondary objective should also be to have parents feel comfortable with the staff in the setting, and this is done by creating a personalised environment for that family. Direct questions such as 'are you religious?' may be deemed inappropriate by some families; however, try leading the conversation by saying:

- 'we love to celebrate different cultures and different holidays here'
- 'are any traditions you have at home that would help to make your child more comfortable in our setting?'
- 'we would love to learn more about special holidays you celebrate at home'
- 'we aim to actively celebrate the multi-cultures that are in the UK here in our setting'.

This opens up a conversation for parents and they are given an option to engage or not.

Step 2: Acting on Information

When parents tell you about their culture, their background, and their traditions, you have a small time frame to act on this information and include it in your setting. Not acting on information is a habit we must avoid at all costs if we are to create an inclusive environment. Multiculturalism in an early years setting is a positive thing and we can all benefit from learning more about the people in our local communities.

Step 3: Bridging the Family

Now that you've learned about individual families and you've begun to integrate their beliefs and their cultures into your school, you have a perfect bridge to invite those families in to be more involved in school culture. This can be done in the following ways:

- Ask parents to come in as mystery readers to share stories from their own countries
- Ask parents to bring dishes from their culture into the setting
- Learn how to cook these things in the setting
- Invite parents to lead a circle time in a presentation on an aspect of their culture
- Ask parents to provide examples of language they use at home and put these in displays in the setting
- Integrate technology and video-call a family from their home and have them teach lessons or engage in class discussions.
- If possible, continue down the technology route and ask families to contact their relatives in another country to arrange a video to be made.
- Alternatively send postcards to a child's family from their home country.
- Ask families to provide photographs of their celebrations and create a family board in the setting.

The simple act of being interested and engaging with someone else's culture is a fantastic tool for creating parent partnership in a school. The UK is a cultural melting-pot and once we start the conversation, we will often find ourselves surprised at where it ends up.

TIME TO THINK:

- Think of five things you would share from your culture if you were asked to.
- Think of five times you've asked parents to share their culture with you.

TIME TO REFLECT:

Could you think of examples easily?
How might you open this partnership further?

Cultural Melting Pots

Once we start to engage parents from diverse backgrounds, we will start to see an increase in cultural dimensions in our settings and this is wonderful. We all currently live in a globalised society, and globalisation is the process by which multiple cultures, languages, and countries come together and work together to create a more effective society. A 'global society' is a society in which all the people of the world have a good deal in common with one another.

TIME TO THINK:

Make a list of all the things that are special to you.
As an example, my list (to name a few) would include:

My wallet, given to me by a very special person
A glass of red (or two) on a Friday night
My kitchen
My books
Chocolate raisins

TIME TO REFLECT:

Review your list and make a note of how the things you like/which are special to you are specific to your culture and how someone from a different cultural background might have a different list. We should also be aware of the things we have in common and the differences we should be aware of.

For example, cultures often include cuisine. We can literally tell which country someone is from if they tell us what their national food is and we all have this element of culture in common; we all have to eat, and we all tend to enjoy eating. So much culture can be shared through a meal and this is something you will likely have in common with someone from a different background. However, a big part of British culture is drinking and someone coming from a more conservative background (Islamic, Jainist, Sikh) likely does not drink at all or sees drinking as a bad thing. If we imagine ourselves at a table right now, we simultaneously have something in common and something that separates us, and how we navigate this is how we create a positive cultural relationship. Have a look at your list: what are the things you think you would have in common with other cultures and what are the things you might need to navigate.

Why Navigate?

We often use the term navigate in relation to other cultures. From my experience working in Asian countries as a British man, I have found that each region of Asia has specific customs, manners, and etiquette that must be observed by people wishing to join in with the culture. I have always believed in a version of the saying *'When in Rome, do as the Romans do.'* How we behave with other cultures is indicative of how culturally competent and aware we are. Integrating into new cultures and understanding diverse cultural protocols can help us to develop parent partnership, child partnership, and communication skills. The responsibility is not the practitioner's alone; this approach must be a two way street. Families and practitioners must both work to make a success within a new cultural dimension. Families who join your setting should be invited to enjoy aspects of British culture too. There is enough space for all of us, and we're all smart enough to learn multiple layers of protocol and how they can work together, and this is why we use the term *navigate*, because no one single side should be favoured over the other, provided we are making space for each other.

This is how we create a cultural melting pot, or as we would say in education, it's how we begin to develop intercultural competence, a theme we have previously explored in Chapter 3. There's no one specific way to organise intercultural competence, but as we explore it in the setting, we will see several benefits for the children in our care.

Specific Challenges to Engaging Families

Today, there is a fear that parents can feel unsupported and unsure of what they need to be doing. This comes as no surprise when legislation, research, public opinion, private connections, and online presences all talk of the best way for children to be raised. Fortunately for practitioners, parents often have a similar set of issues related to raising a child and related to education. In my experience, these have been related to the following areas:

1. Whether the focus should be on educational practices **OR** letting their kids be kids.
2. If they should feel guilt for having full-time jobs as well as children.
3. If they're doing enough at home to support a child's education.
4. If their child isn't developing comparatively to someone else's child.
5. How parents could learn to think more like educators and keep education going at home.

This is by no means an exhaustive list of issues that parents face and which cultural background a family comes from will determine which issues a family is willing to open up about. Our first responsibility is to work with patience. Powell and Goouch (2012) found that, in England, almost half of all babies were in some form of daycare setting and this level of children in settings (both informal and formal) means a staggering amount of parent communication is required. Through this, we can expect to see specific issues which pose barriers to parent partnership. Let's explore these together and, as practitioners, start to think of solution to these issues.

Lapse in Communication

Most issues faced by early years practitioners could be resolved if the communication channels are open and effective. The key issue for a practitioner working with any family new to the UK is that the breakdown in communication could be simply a language barrier as opposed to an effective breakdown. An effective breakdown might be defined as a breakdown in the relationship between the family, a disagreement over practice, or a general inability to form a bond. This in itself is a separate issue from a communication breakdown. Your role in this exchange is to ensure that your communication channel is always open and that you find ways to communicate effectively with the family. This expectation works both ways and you should make it clear to families that communicating clearly with the setting is important if we are to understand one another, which inevitably is the best thing for the child in our care.

Lack of Time

A lapse in communication is often caused by having a lack of time to communicate with parents. Giving time does not just mean making phone calls or sending emails, it means being available to the families should they need to meet, should you need to voice some concerns or celebrate some successes, or even time to come and explore the setting as it's developing throughout the year. Taking time to add a rich element of interaction with the family is a very important method of engaging a family within the setting. It builds trust, and moreover, for an EAL family, it might just help them settle into the UK a little bit more easily. Families can tell when we're rushing, and often when we rush our interactions with the family are sloppy and of poor quality.

Conflicting Cultures

We explore the prospect of culture in great detail in another chapter, but it's worth mentioning here. Culture plays such an important part in all of our lives and may play a role in a family's view of child development and education. In Asian countries, for example, play-based pedagogy is still a new venture for many families, whereas in the West it is the norm. This can create a conflict of culture between the setting and the family and practitioners should be patient as families adjust to the reality of British education. Again, having a conversation with families before they join the setting could alleviate any symptoms of conflicting culture such as aforementioned language barriers or misunderstandings.

Practitioners really must make an effort to understand the cultural heritage and background of the people in their care and this includes the families. Families should be offered bridges into the setting's culture. This shared cultural exchange can alleviate further conflict in the future.

Conflicting Expectations

In line with conflicting culture, family expectations of education are also likely to be different from what we are used to in the UK. Families from different cultures will have different ideas regarding rules, mode of instruction, group values, and discipline. This could create a conflict as children go home and talk about their school day. A way to alleviate this is to ask the family what their expectations are in these areas before they join the setting.

Roles and Responsibilities

Different cultures may also have different views on the role of the teacher and the power a teacher should have over a child. Often teachers have specific education and knowledge that prepares them for child development and parents more often than not don't have this knowledge. This creates a power imbalance between the family and the setting as parents may be seen as customers as opposed to active participants in their child's learning. It is essential to overcome this and create a joint approach to child development; both parent and teacher are responsible for the child and should look at each other as a team. However, also be aware that some parents will fully expect teachers to perform their roles without any input from parents. Our role as practitioners is to find a balance.

Family History

A family's previous experience with schools and education may also be a factor for disagreement and this could be for two reasons. Firstly, a family may come to you with a pre-imagined ideal quality education because they were fond of their previous school. Alternatively, a family may come to you distrustful because they have had a bad experience. Talk to the family and determine which of these is the case. Communicate with the family about their needs and their expectations; explain clearly how you will meet these.

Staff Movements

How staff present themselves to parents, and how they are moved around the setting throughout times when parents are present, is an important consideration for engaging families. Take note of the fact that when children go home, they will talk about their favourite teachers, and that won't always be the senior teacher in the room. However, senior teachers are often the ones facing families; they are essentially the face of the class. If a less senior member of staff is often given cleaning up duties, or menial duties during collection time, parents won't get to know them in the same way they get to know the senior member. All staff should be the face of the room because we are a collaborative team of practitioners. Consider best practice for future interactions with parents and how it will make parents feel more comfortable with the staffing in the setting.

Furthermore, staff turnover must be avoided at all costs. Schools die because of staff turnover. When a school is unable to maintain staff for a solid year, this is very indicative of the kind of work environment the school has created and parents will see staff turnover as a transparent message that the school is not a positive environment for their child. It is the duty of managers to create a happy workspace for their team. Happy staff will have happy children.

TIME TO REFLECT:

- Which of the above issues have you worked with in your time as an educator?
- What are some solutions/strategies you could put in place to avoid these issues?

Parent Partnership Ideas

There is no single way to approach parent partnership and there's no easy fix when things go wrong. We all know this because we often work with children who need comprehensive long-term strategies to maintain their educational practice. Parent partnership can also require long-term comprehensive strategies. Take a look at the following top ten ideas for parent partnership adapted from the work of Martin (2006) and see how you could incorporate these ideas into your practice:

1. Negotiate what partnership means, and how it might be used to support family and child.
2. Find out what parent involvement is at home and reflect this in the setting.

3. Ask families to provide support in areas they are already interested in; for example, a family with a love of art can recommend good art projects.
4. Involve parents as decision-makers.
5. Email newsletters and include questions or invite families to vote on decisions being made in the setting.
6. Share photos and retell observations with parents before writing them up as a learning story.
7. Create parent–teacher contracts which define the specialities each person brings to the education of the child.
8. Inquire what the parent thinks about the information you pass on to them. Avoid giving advice, labelling, or in any way sounding like an expert!
9. Invite families to present ideas by using questions rather than statements.
10. Communicate about children's learning interests and daily experiences, as this is arguably some of the most important information.

 TIME TO THINK:

Make your own list of the top ten strategies you could put in place to support parent partnership in your setting.

 TIME TO REFLECT:

Share with your team your successes and your failures in parent partnership. Only through acknowledging our difficulties can we hope to achieve success.

Finally...

Be yourself! That's why you got hired in the first place!

The reader should now have a broader idea on support strategies to put into place for the families of EAL children. Chapter 8, our final chapter, will help us to explore who we are as teachers and how we can further our own practice to reach positive outcomes.

FURTHER READING TO SUPPORT CHAPTER 7

1. Featherstone, S. (2017). *An Anthology of Educational Thinkers: Putting Theory into Practice in the Early Years*. London: Bloomsbury.

Conclusion

In this chapter, we will bring together the key ideas of this book, and how we might work to improve ourselves as practitioners of the early years. We will explore the teaching standards of the early years and how we can use these to work reflectively on our own practice.

Introduction

Take a minute to read the poem 'Search for my Tongue by Sujata Bhatt'; it's easy to find online if you have the time. Don't just skip it because it seems unnecessary or unhelpful in relation to our work, but really take a minute to reflect on the words of the poem. Sujata Bhatt explores here deep questions about the connected nature of culture, identity, and immigration. She explores the difficulty of self-expression a person experiences when they speak a foreign language, especially when that foreign language dominates and takes over from their own, and the imagery in the poem reflects the language and culture journey experienced by our EAL children when they join a predominantly English-speaking setting.

We have to remember that when a child is coming to a setting to learn our culture and our language, there is a distinct possibility the child is simultaneously being removed from their own culture and identity. 'Search for my Tongue' explores this notion in beautiful detail, and the words of the poem can be so much more applicable to the experiences a child has when removed from the safety and comfort of their home language.

DOI: 10.4324/9781003190219-9

We have discussed this in other chapters, and we've explored how we might better support children when they're removed from their initial support system, but I implore practitioners, when in doubt, to reflect back on 'Search for my Tongue' when trying to think of the struggle and difficulty a child may have as they grow within the early years in search of their identity.

Standards of Teaching

Within the EYFS there is a set of teaching standards that practitioners should regularly be reflecting on in order to ensure that their practice is maintained to a high standard. The teaching standards provide a guideline for how practitioners can bring more to their class and how they can better equip themselves to support children in the early years. In this final chapter, we will explore the teaching standards together and look at how we can apply these teaching standards to support EAL children.

The following is inspired by and adapted from DfES, 2013. *Teachers' Standards (Early Years)*, National College for Teaching and Leadership.

Standard 1 – 'Set high expectations which inspire, motivate and challenge all children'

We've talked at length in this book of setting high expectations for children with EAL, but it's important to understand that these expectations are not meant to impose difficulties on children in our care but should be used as a way to encourage that child to learn English in an appropriate time frame. Inevitably, learning English is the only way for an EAL child to have access to frameworks and curricula as they continue their education.

It's also important to remember that the same high expectation should be put on practitioners to provide rich learning environments for children. One set of high expectations cannot exist without the other and practitioners should at all times be pushing themselves to create an environment that supports the children in their care.

Children should also be motivated to learn, and this includes taking a keen interest in their interests and building on these to create challenges that further the learning environment.

TIME TO REFLECT:

Write down five examples of a time when you have worked above and beyond to inspire, motivate, and challenge all children.

TIME TO THINK:

Now write down five new ideas that you could import into the setting after reading this book, add these into your planning and start putting things into practice as soon as possible. Remember, with EAL children it's important to have strategies in place sooner rather than later.

Standard 2 – 'Promote good progress and outcomes by children'

Working with children is not just being in a setting of early learners but taking on the responsibility for their learning and their earliest educational outcomes. This should be taken seriously, especially as early education is often not looked upon as being as important as primary or secondary education. Research shows, however, that the early years are a focal point for our later academic and personal achievements. There's a reason the early years are called the formative years and the responsibility we have for progress and outcomes for children is incredibly high.

For EAL children we are also adopting the responsibility of their language development and future abilities. Given that the children in your care will need English to be educated, to be social, and to get through the day to day of living in the UK, this responsibility is heightened for any practitioner who has EAL children in their care. English itself is a lingua franca and this means that when a child learns how to speak English, they can communicate with the world at large, with the many children and adults who have also been exposed to/learned English.

Having key attachments with these children, communicating effectively with these children, helping a child to develop confidence, these are all part of the standard of care that you should be offering when a child is in your setting. But you're not alone; the great thing about standard 2 is that there is a team of people who are responsible for the progress and outcomes of children, and these include parents, carers, and other teachers, and as a team we can work on having the best outcomes for children.

TIME TO THINK:

- Thinking of the EAL children are in your class, are you confident that you have provided the best outcomes to these children?
- Have you reached a group consensus with the other people in the life of that child on the care needs of that child?
- Is there more you could do for each individual EAL child in your care?

TIME TO REFLECT:

Consider each EAL child in your class. What strategy could you put in place tomorrow to better support their confidence, their social skills, and their connection to you and to their peers?

Share your reflections with other practitioners so they too might understand how better to work with children in their settings. Remember, we're a community!

Standard 3 – 'Demonstrate good knowledge of early learning and EYFS'

The EYFS can be a complicated and expansive framework that encompasses the earliest experiences of a child's early life. In education, there is often a culture of 'sweeping things under the rug', assuming a child will just 'pick up a set of skills', and now more than ever, a culture of 'catching up on missed learning opportunities'. I don't judge anyone who has these thoughts, because it's safe to say we are all guilty of this behaviour at some point in our teaching careers and the reasons for this are often that we are overworked, over-encumbered, or simply not present in the moment when learning is taking place. Adding to this is the need for practitioners to remain up to date with ideas on best practice, and with the EYFS itself.

One key way a practitioner can remain present in the moment is to ensure that time is taken (or given by the employer) for simple research purposes. This time would apply to your continuing professional development and should be a time in the week when staff can continue their studies in the field of education.

Practitioners should never look at their qualifications as 'completed' simply because a certificate was awarded. Research grows and changes constantly and it is our duty to follow these changes and implement them into our practice. This is especially poignant for the EAL children in your class as we continue to learn and recognise the changing needs of children from multilingual and multicultural backgrounds.

Time to Act

Go into your setting at the next possible opportunity and make one tangible change that you think will benefit a child with EAL.

TIME TO REFLECT:

Did you see a positive impact on your change? How could you continue to make additions/evolutions to your class to benefit an EAL child?

Standard 4 – 'Plan education and care taking account of the needs of all children'

As we need to plan for the strengths of EAL children, it's also important to ensure that children with EAL are not sidelined in comparison with their English-speaking peers. We have explored this phenomenon in the book in previous chapters, and again I will say, it's important that children are not being expected to engage in 'pick up' culture. All children must be planned for in a unique way given that the framework we use is underpinned by the unique child approach, and practitioners of the early years must focus on key differentiation that will benefit children with EAL.

 TIME TO THINK:

Create a piece of planning for a simple activity, and practise differentiating for children whose English is not as developed as the other children in your class.

 TIME TO REFLECT:

Review your previous planning: is there key evidence of differentiation in this planning?

If not, get in some practice by adding differentiation for EAL children.

Standard 5 – 'Adapt education and care to respond to the strengths and needs of all children'

Standard 5 is particularly important when taking into account the educational needs of the EAL child and the reason for this is; while we have spent this entire book discussing the wellbeing of children with EAL, we must be reminded that being EAL is not the only thing that makes up these particular children. EAL children, like all children, are complex creatures made up of unique needs and wants and interests. When we plan in the EYFS, it is essential for us to understand what the unique needs of each child are, but also the unique strengths. We have explored in detail how to better support the needs of an EAL child, but now let's think of some simple ways to explore what a child's strengths are.

1. Observe the child in the setting and determine which areas of learning they are excelling in, maybe the EAL child is a fascinated artist or master of motor skills.
2. Gain a brief student profile from the family/previous teachers of the child, what activities is the child most likely to engage in at home or in class?
3. Explore activities in class with the child and see which ones produce the longest engagement time.
4. Provide more opportunities for unique interests.

Practitioners must avoid looking at the child only in terms of their language and must work to see the child as a whole.

Standard 6 – 'Make accurate and productive use of assessment'

Assessment in the early years is an important part of the learning cycle; *observe, assess, plan*. Without observation, we're left with little evidence of what's happening in the class, and practitioners should consider the following methods of observation in order to get the most productive examples for assessment:

1. Spontaneous Observation
2. Sociogram
3. Running Narrative Record
4. Media Record
5. Work Examples
6. Time Samples

In many settings practitioners fall back on spontaneous observation because, in truth, it is the easiest form of observation, we often struggle to find time to do anything that takes a little longer such as sociograms or narrative records, but by omitting these forms of observations, practitioners are realistically unable to make productive use of assessment. Productive here means that what we observe can be used to build upon to support children's access to the early years framework. When we have a variety of examples of how children are learning, only then can we assess what that learning means, so it is essential that in your setting time is put aside for practitioners to conduct a variety of observations.

As we've discussed, most areas of the EYFS can be assessed within the child's first language, however communication, language, and literacy must be assessed in English. Only with accurate and appropriate levels of observation can practitioners make accurate assessments of a child's development in these key areas. As much as we should respect a child's native language and native culture, a child growing up in the UK needs English and it is a practitioner's responsibility to observe and assess their development here as a priority.

TIME TO THINK:

Review the records you keep of a child's learning during their time in your care (learning Journeys, children's portfolios etc.) and determine what the key makeup of these is. Is it a variety of observational methods or is it mainly spontaneous observation?

TIME TO REFLECT:

How could your setting better support you to make sure you can make productive use of observation and assessment?

Share these ideas whenever possible with leadership so that you are better able to provide a quality education for all children, including EAL children.

Standard 7 – 'Safeguard and promote the welfare of children, and provide a safe learning environment'

When we think of safeguarding, we often jump to an immediate conclusion in the early years: physical or sexual abuse. Safeguarding, however, denotes the measures that we've put in place to protect the health, wellbeing and human rights of children in our care. It also requires a higher responsibility of practitioners to make sure that children are free from abuse, harm, and neglect. Practitioners should have access to the policies and procedures file on site that provides information on the settings plans to support the welfare of children. As we're planning, we have to take into account all children in our care and it's important that we don't neglect those who need additional help, especially EAL children who might not be able to access the setting, the framework, and your support as easily as other children in your care.

By encouraging native language and promoting an 'every child' culture in the setting, we are promoting the welfare of children. By allowing children to take safe risks, we are promoting welfare, and when we explore multiculturalism in a setting, we are again promoting the wellbeing of all children in our care. Sustaining this environment is of equal importance, which means working in coalition with children and other practitioners to make sure that as the framework we're using develops, so does the provision for children. EAL children should feel warm and safe in the setting and there should be policies in place that support both the EAL child as well as the family of the EAL child.

TIME TO THINK:

Are there existing policies and procedures in your setting that protect the welfare and support the safety of children coming from multicultural backgrounds?

TIME TO REFLECT:

Have you encountered any situations that you could share with others where the safety of an EAL or immigrant child was at risk because of their status?

Standard 8 – 'Fulfil wider professional responsibilities'

When thinking about your wider professional responsibilities, ask yourself the following set of questions:

- Am I sharing my knowledge and information with my peers?
- Do I generally contribute to a workplace where we can cooperate with each other?
- Do I support multiculturalism and inclusivity in the setting?
- Do I stand up to prejudice such as racial discrimination when I see it?
- Do I take responsibility for not only the children in my care but for the care of the children in the whole setting?
- Have I made it part of my daily routine to learn about the changes that take place in a child's home environment?
- Have I incorporated and included families into my daily practice?
- Would I be considered a professional team player by my team?

It's important to note that standard 8 does not mean taking responsibility for other people's work and other people's roles, but we should all understand the role standard 8 plays in settings that take pride in the holistic approach. Standard 8 does not ask you to take on the weight of an entire setting, but it does expect all of us within a setting to view the care and education of children as something we're all involved in. Whether you are a manager, a room leader, or practitioner, the care of each and every child is your responsibility and by fulfilling our own professional responsibilities, we are better equipped to work as a team, which in turn will create a richer and more progressive learning environment for all children, including children with EAL.

TIME TO THINK:

Answer the following questions:

1. What training or support could my team use to make their daily work easier?
2. What could I do to be a better teammate?
3. Who in this setting do I think could support me better in my work and in turn, who do I think I could offer more support to?
4. If I could change one thing about my daily experience what would it be?

Try to share your ideas with leadership, but always remember to be patient. Things don't often change overnight and really, they're not expected to. The best approach for early years settings is often a gradual and structured approach that supports a smooth transition for children, so take pleasure in the small victories, and continue to work within the best interests of the child.

As we've explored the teaching standards a little more, you will have noticed that there's more call for reflection than in other chapters and this is because, as we conclude with this book, I want practitioners to think of reflection and reflective practice above all as a tool for supporting the well-being of the children in our care.

Reflective Practice

One of the most useful tools for the early years practitioner is reflection. Reflection is not just the practice of looking back at lesson planning and deciding whether or not it could be improved, but it is the practice of understanding how our behaviour, our interactions and how our teaching impacted the daily lives of our children. Reflection is often seen as a way to fix problems; however, I disagree with this and think reflection should be used to celebrate your successes and improve your practice where possible. As you've read this book you've been expected to reflect on numerous occasions, and this is because reflective practice is something you should include in your daily lives.

Reflection doesn't just apply to work either but is a fantastic method to understand your own wellbeing and as I've said, you can't pour from an empty cup. Your own mental personal and emotional wellbeing is just as important as that of the children in your care.

Here we will explore a number of amazing opportunities for practitioners to reflect broadly and I would highly advise that practitioners incorporate this type of reflection into their daily practice to make sure that they are keeping on top of their own needs.

1. Self-Questioning

In the same way that we do spontaneous observation, practitioners should engage in spontaneous self-questioning. Practitioners should engage in activities with children so as to see the usefulness of provocations and areas of continuous provision in the room. We might find ourselves reflecting on what we see. In the same way we use post-its to write down these things, we should write down the questions and the answers to those questions as they come into our heads. These may include:

- Am I seeing evidence of sustained shared thinking?
- Am I seeing evidence of sustained engagement?
- Are there opportunities for joint attention?
- Have I evolved my environment adequately to support the needs of the children?
- Am I interfering or interacting?
- Is there more I could do?
- Is my environment inviting and engaging or is it overwhelming?

These are just a small example of questions we tend to ask ourselves throughout the day and if we take note of these and keep them in a safe space where we can go back and reflect, we are truly creating a reflective environment for ourselves.

2. Student Questionnaire

Student questionnaires are a fantastic way of engaging children in the learning environment. Obviously, within early years, especially in the lower end of the framework, actual questionnaires are unrealistic, and even in the older age groups, an actual questionnaire might seem inappropriate in a constructivist environment. However, in supporting children with English as an additional language, practitioners might enjoy bringing some conversation time into a circle time, and this conversation could relate to a child's fulfillment during activities in class.

Consider planning for the week, consider children's interests, and consider most of all how those two things should go together within the EYFS framework. I have found great success by simply asking children the following questions:

1. Which activities do you want to do?
2. Was there an activity that we did last week that you'd like to try again?
3. If I could put out three resources right now, what would you want to play with?
4. What did you not enjoy? Is there anything you found boring?
5. Did you enjoy (insert specific activity)?

If you use this method consistently in the setting it's highly likely that children will come to realise that their opinions and the things that they say have meaning. Doing this on a weekly basis can help to create a consistently child-led, teacher-guided approach within the setting and create rich learning language opportunities for EAL children in the setting.

3. Classroom Recordings

As much as people hate recordings, seeing yourself in action is one of the best and most effective ways of reflecting on your own practice. When we watch ourselves teach, we may be surprised by the positives that we bring to the room, but equally we may be surprised at our own behaviour. Old habits die hard, and this is no different in teaching and as teaching has evolved, so must we evolve to meet the needs of our children. Take the time to record your own teaching and reflect on what you see. Think of the following:

- Is my body language open and accessible?
- Is my tone of voice kind considerate?
- What would I change about the way I'm interacting?
- What do I think I did really well?
- Was there anything I did that made me feel uncomfortable?
- Did I see reactions from the children that I perhaps wouldn't want to see again?
- On which occasions did children respond really well to my behaviour?

Remember, as much as it's important to admit mistakes and to fix problems, it's also important to celebrate the previous successes!

4. Journaling

Journaling might not seem like something you have time for every day, but I can say with 100 per cent honesty that journaling helped my practice immensely and the reason for this was my inability to pinpoint which parts of my day gave me a little bit of anxiety, and which parts of my day I felt that I could have done better. When journaling, I always found it best to be in a quiet space but also was happy to do it in a staff room during coffee time and all I simply did was write. I didn't give myself a task, and I didn't give myself any pressure. I just started writing to see what would come out, and this is the same advice I would give to you. You are likely to surprise yourself with the things that you write down, but the best outcome for journaling is that it might help you pinpoint things you didn't realise. Furthermore, I often found that once my thoughts were out of my head, I was able to calm my anxieties.

5. Peer Observation

Peer observation starts with the notion that we can ask our colleagues to join us in the setting. When we engage in peer observation, we can ask for the following things;

- Feedback on our teaching and pedagogy
- Feedback on the environment
- Feedback on a specific activity or area of learning

It's often best with peer observation to discuss what you want the peer to look for before they come into the room; this way the observation material that you receive is rich and will provide you with opportunities for self-development.

It's important when we do peer observation that we ask someone we know who can help us, someone who's experienced in the field or in the task at hand. The first rule I often teach with peer-to-peer observation is that you must throw away your pride and be open to accepting the feedback that others have provided, providing that feedback is constructive. As long as you feel you can learn from something, it's important that you take it on board and work towards a positive outcome. Reflective practice means accepting that we can always improve our own pedagogy. But do keep in mind that if you disagree with something someone says, it's important to speak up and explain your practice. Observers don't know everything, so it's important to communicate to fill in the gaps. Peer observation is not about lecturing; it should be an open discussion with aims to move forward. Remember, if someone in the setting knows more than you or is more experienced than you, you should see them as an opportunity for self-development. Equally you should offer yourself as a peer observer if you are available to help others, because this feeds back into the standards of teaching, such as fulfilling the wider ethos of the setting.

6. Cooperating with Peers

As we go through peer observation, we should also be working in cooperation with our wider peers in the setting. It doesn't benefit a setting to have two or three teachers working on reflection and development if the other teachers are excluded from that development. Peer cooperation benefits settings in a number of ways. Peers are able to learn from one another, and further discover things about pedagogy and practice that they maybe haven't experienced before. This is particularly useful for cross-age groups because when practitioners spend a lot of time in their particular age group, they might lose touch with practices that still could be relevant to their teaching.

This is particularly effective for EAL children because practitioners working with EAL children may need to revert to easier practices before moving forward. Excellent methods of cooperating with peers include:

- Formal staff meetings
- CPD Sessions
- Informal meetings
- Staff show & tell
- Staff guest presenters

It's important to find ways to engage with all staff and motivate them whether they're trainees or qualified.

7. Classroom Mirrors (Literal Reflections!)

This may seem like a strange addition to reflective practice, but reflective practice can come in micro and macro forms, and this would be one of the microforms. We know that our communication is heavily influenced by our body language and facial expression, and now more than ever how we use our faces has become increasingly important. For a long time, face masks have been a part of our daily lives and what effect these have had is yet to be seen; as we transition out of the regulations requiring face masks, it's likely we will see a change to how our facial expressions are registered by those in our care.

When we're increasingly busy, particularly towards the end of the day, how we react visually can be very transparent to a child in our care. Even if we answer a question asked of us, when it's accompanied with an eye-roll or a sigh, the bond between ourselves and the child in our care is damaged. This is particularly important for a child who cannot understand your language and is relying on your physical cues to understand the flow of the conversation.

Having a mirror/multiple mirrors in the classroom is not only great for imaginative play and making the room seem larger but is a great reminder to check our body language as we go about our days.

8. *Mindful Reflection*

And our final idea for reflective practice is one of my personal favourites, and that is *being mindful*. Mindfulness comes from a place of peace, when we can settle down and be at one with our thoughts. As a practitioner of the early years myself, I know for a fact that many of us don't have time when we can be peaceful and at one with our thoughts because we're often thinking about the numerous learning opportunities, work responsibilities, and personal responsibilities that make up our lives. Taking some time to reflect on practice is incredibly important, and one of the best ways to do this is to be mindful.

To be mindful, generally we want to follow these guidelines:

1. Find a space that is cool, comfortable, and quiet.
2. If you like, play a soft piece of music or create an ambiance to take your mind out of the place you're in.
3. Focus on your breathing, focus on the way you feel, empty your mind of all of those thoughts and try to just be at one in the moment.
4. Breathe deeply and slowly and try to calm down any feelings of stress, anxiety, or pressure.
5. If your mind wanders, let it wander, but don't let it wander to a stressful place.
6. Stay like this for as long as it's possible (it might be best to try it at home).

When we're being mindful of ourselves, we might realise or recognise something in our own minds that we don't expect; this is a powerful method of reflective practice and one that can be transitioned and used for an EAL child who may need time also to be at one in their own mind, whilst they're adapting to a setting that doesn't use their language.

In Conclusion

I hope you've taken something from this book, and even if you've learned or considered just one thing that helps a child in your care then the book has achieved its purpose. I also hope that the explorations of culture, identity, and immigration can help you as practitioners to reflect on the realities faced by many of the children in your care, especially those who may not be native to the UK or whose families may not be native to the UK.

In my opinion, only when we act as members of a global society can we really benefit those people in our care, both child and family alike, and simply by picking up this book it seems that you maybe have the same perspective.

Best of luck in your continuing careers as teachers and practitioners!

The reader should now have a broader idea of the experience an EAL child has in the setting, and hopefully has gained more insight into how they might better support the children in their care.

FURTHER READING TO SUPPORT CHAPTER 8

1. Burnham, L. (2016). *How to Be an Outstanding Early Years Practitioner.* London: Bloomsbury.

Bibliography

Aukrust, V. (2007). Young children acquiring second language vocabulary in preschool group-time: Does amount, diversity, and discourse complexity of teacher talk matter? *Journal of Research in Childhood Education.*

Bandura, A. (1977). *Social Learning Theory.* Englewood Cliffs, NJ: Prentice-Hall.

Barone, D. and Xu, S. H. (2008). *Literacy Instruction for English Language Learners Pre-K–2.* New York: Guilford Press.

Bates, E. and MacWhinney, B. (1982). Functionalist approaches to grammar. In Wanner, E. and Gleitman, L. (eds) *Language Acquisition: The State of the Art.* Cambridge: Cambridge University Press.

Bialystok, E. (2001). *Bilingualism in Development: Language, Literacy and Cognition.* Cambridge : Cambridge University Press

Bilmes, J. (2012). *Beyond Behavior Management: The Six Life Skills Children Need,* 2nd ed. St. Paul, MN: Redleaf.

Bloom, L. (1993). *The Transition from Infancy to Language: Acquiring the Power of Expression.* New York: Cambridge University Press.

Boroditsky, L. (2017). *How Language Shapes the Way We Think.* [video] Directed by L. Borditsky. TED New Orleans, Louisiana.

Bourne, J. (2001). Doing 'what comes naturally': How the discourses and routines of teachers' practice constrain opportunities for bilingual support in UK primary schools. *Language and Education,* 15(4).

Bovey, T. and Strain, P. (2005). Strategies for increasing peer social interactions: Prompting and acknowledgment. *What Works Briefs.* Center on the Social and Emotional Foundations for Early Learning. Available at: http://csefel.vanderbilt.edu/briefs/wwb17.pdf.

Brewer, S. and Cutting, A. (2001). *A Child's World.* London: Headline.

Brooker, L. (2005). Learning to be a child: Cultural diversity and early years ideology. In Yelland, N. (ed.) *Critical Issues in Early Childhood Education*. Maidenhead: Open University Press.

Bruner, J. S. (1960). *The Process of Education*. Cambridge, MA: Harvard University Press.

Cambourne, B. (1988). *The Whole Story*. Warwick, UK: Scholastic Publishing.

Cameron, L., Moon, J., and Bygate, M. (1996). Language development of bilingual pupils in the mainstream: How do pupils and teachers use language? *Language and Education*. 10(4), 221–236.

Carlo, M. S., August, D., McLaughlin, B., Snow, C., Dressler, C., Lippman, D. N., ...White, C. E. (2004). Closing the gap: Addressing the vocabulary needs of English-language learners in bilingual and mainstream classrooms. *Reading Research Quarterly*, 39(2), 188–215.

Chang, H.N.-L. (1993). *Affirming Children's Roots: Cultural and Linguistic Diversity in Early Care and Education*. San Francisco, CA: California Tomorrow.

Chomsky, N. (1959). A review of B. F. Skinner's *Verbal Behavior. Language*, 35, 26–58

Chomsky, N. (1964). *Current Issues in Linguistic Theory*. The Hague: Mouton.

Christakis, D., Gilkerson, J., Richards, A., Zimmerman, J., Garrison, M., Dongxin, X., Gray, S., and Yapanel, U. (2009). Audible television and decreased adult words, infant vocalisations and conversational turntaking. *Archives of Pediatrics and Adolescent Medicine*, 163(6) (June): 554–558.

Christie, J. and Roskos, K. (2006). Standards, science, and the role of play in early literacy education. In D. G. Singer, R.M. Golinkoff, and K. Hirsh-Pasek (eds), *Play=learning: How Play Motivates and Enhances Children's Cognitive and Social-emotional Growth* (pp. 57–73). New York: Oxford University Press.

Clarke, P. (1992). *English as a 2nd Language in Early Childhood*. Richmond, Victoria: FKA Multicultural Resource Centre.

Cline, T. and Frederickson, N. (Eds) (1996). *Curriculum Related Assessment, Cummins and Bilingual Children*. Clevedon: Multilingual Matters.

Cummins, J. (1984). *Bilingualism and Special Education*. Clevedon: Multilingual Matters.

Cummins, J. (2000). *Language, Power and Pedagogy*. Clevedon: Multilingual Matters.

Davies, N., (2012). *NALDIC | EAL guidance | Pupils learning EAL*. [online] Naldic.org.uk. Available at: https://www.naldic.org.uk/eal-teaching-and -learning/outline-guidance/pupils/

Dionne, G., Dale, S. P., Boivin, M., and Plomin, R. (2003). Genetic evidence for bidirectional effects of early lexical and grammatical development. *Child Development*, 74(2), 394–412.

DfES, (2007). *Departmental Report*. Crown Copyright.

DfES (2013). *Teachers' Standards (Early Years)*. National College for Teaching and Leadership.

DfES. (2021). https://assets.publishing.service.gov.uk/government/uploads/ system/uploads/attachment_data/file/974907/EYFS_framework_-_March _2021.pdf

Dombro, A.L., J. Jablon, and C. Stetson. (2011). *Powerful Interactions: How to Connect with Children to Extend Their Learning*. Washington, DC: National Association for the Education of Young Children (NAEYC).

Drury, Rose (2007). *Young Bilingual Learners at Home and School: Researching Multilingual Voices*. Stoke on Trent: Trentham Books.

Duffy, R. (2008). "Are Feelings Fixable?" *Exchange*, 30(6), 87–90.

Edu, Harvard. (2019). *Toxic Stress*. [online] Center on the Developing Child at Harvard University. Available at: https://developingchild.harvard.edu/ science/key-concepts/toxic-stress/

Elliot, R. (2003). Sharing care and education: Parents' perspectives. *Australian Journal of Early Childhood*, 28(4), 14–21.

Ferjan Ramirez, N. (2017). *Creating Bilingual Minds*. [video] Directed by N. Ferjan Ramirez. TedxLjubljana: Tedx.

Fogel, A. (1993). *Developing through Relationships: Origins of Communication, Self, and Culture*. Chicago, IL: University of Chicago Press.

Ford, K. (2010). 8 Strategies for Preschool ELLs' Language and Literacy Development. Available at: https://www.luc.edu/media/lucedu/ education/pdfs/languagematters/Sp16_Strauts&Seidler_handout_8-St rategies-for-Preschool-ELLs.pdf

Franson, C. (2008). *NALDIC | EAL guidance | Bilingualism and Second Language Acquisition*. [online] Naldic.org.uk. Available at: https://www .naldic.org.uk/Resources/NALDIC/Initial%20Teacher%20Education/ Documents/bilingualism.pdf

Gaertner, B., Spinrad, T., and Eisenberg, N. (2008). Focused attention in toddlers. *Infant Child Development*.

Gillanders, Cristina. (2007). An English-speaking prekindergarten teacher for young Latino children: Implications of the teacher–child relationship on second language learning. *Early Childhood Education Journal*, 35, 47–54.

Gillborn, David and Mirza, Heidi. (2000). Educational inequality: Mapping race, class and gender: A synthesis of research evidence. Office for Standards in Education. https://dera.ioe.ac.uk//4428/2/Educational_inequality_mapping _race%2C_class_and_gender_%28PDF_format%29.pdf

Golinkoff, R. M. (1986). I beg your pardon?: The preverbal negotiation of failed messages. *Journal of Child Language*, 13(3), 455–476.

Gordon, A.M. and K.W. Browne. (2014). *Beginnings and Beyond: Foundations in Early Childhood Education*, 9th ed. Belmont, CA: Cengage.

Graff, F. (2020). In babies, crucial neural connections happen before age three. [online] Science.unctv.org. Available at: https://science.unctv.org/ content/reportersblog/babies-neural-connections

Greater London Authority. (2020). *Migration Indicators*. London: GLA.

Han, M., Moore, N., Vukelich, C., and Buell, M. (2011). Does play make a difference? How play intervention affects the vocabulary learning of at-risk preschoolers. *American Journal of Play*, 3(1), 82–104.

Hay, J. F., Pelucchi, B., Graf Estes, K., and Saffran, J. R. (2001). Linking sounds to meanings: Infant statistical learning in a natural language. *Cognitive Psychology*, 63(2), 93–106.

Hayes, C. (2016). *Language, Literacy and Communication in the Early Years*. St Albans: Critical Publishing.

Hirsh-Pasek, K., Golinkoff, R. M., Berk, L. E., and Singer, D. G. (2009). *A Mandate for Playful Learning in Preschool: Presenting the Evidence*. New York: Oxford University Press.

Hoff, E., Core, C., Place, S., Rumiche, R., Senor, M., and Parra, M. (2012). Dual language exposure and early bilingual development. *Journal of Child Language*, 39(1), 1–27.

Houston, D. M. and Jusczyk, P. W. (2000). The role of talker-specific information in word segmentation by infants. *Journal of Experimental Psychology: Human Perception and Performance*, 26(5), 1570–1582.

Hurtado, N., Marchman, V. A., and Fernald, A. (2008). Does input influence update? Links between maternal talk, processing speed and vocabulary size in Spanish-learning children. *Developmental Science*, 11(6), 31–39.

Hyson, M. (2004). *The Emotional Development of Young Children: Building an Emotion-Centered Curriculum*, 2nd ed. New York: Teachers College Press.

Konishi, H., Kanero, J., Freemand, M. R., Michnick Golinoff, R., and Hirsh-Pasek, K. (2014). Six principles of language development: Implications for second language learners. *Developmental Neuropsychology*, 39(5), 404–420.

Kuhl, P. K., Tsao, F. M., and Liu, H. M. (2003). Foreign-language experience in infancy: Effects of short-term exposure and social interaction on phonetic learning. *Proceedings of the National Academy of Sciences*, 100(15), 9096–9101.

Lynch, M. (2016). What is culturally responsive pedagogy? [online] *The Edvocate*. Available at: https://www.theedadvocate.org/what-is-culturally -responsive-pedagogy/#:~:text=Culturally%20responsive%20pedagogy %20is%20divided,dimension%2C%20and%20the%20instructional %20dimension.

Macilroy, T. (n.d.). The holistic development of a child during the early years. [online] Empowered Parents. Available at: https://empoweredparents.co/ holistic-development/

Martin-Jones, M. and Saxena, M. (2003). Bilingual resources and 'funds of knowledge' for teaching and learning in multi-ethnic classrooms in Britain. In Creese, A. and Martin, P. (eds) *Multilingual Classroom Ecologies*. Clevedon: Multilingual Matters.

Martin, S. (2006). Opportunities for parent partnership and advocacy in early years services in Ireland. *New Zealand Research in Early Childhood Education*, 9, 15–31.

McClellan, D. and Katz, L. (2001). Assessing Young Children's Social Competence. ERIC Digest. Available at: https://files.eric.ed.gov/fulltext/ ED450953.pdf

McGrath, W.H. (2007). Ambivalent partners: Power, trust and partnership in relationships between mothers and teachers in a full-time child care centre. *Teachers' College Record*, 109(6), 1401–1422.

Mehl, Matthias, Vazire, Simine, Ramírez-Esparza, Nairán, Slatcher, Richard, and Pennebaker, James. (2007). Are women really more talkative than men?. *Science*, 317(5834), 82. DOI:10.1126/science.1139940

Mitchell, L. and Brooking, K. (2007). First NZCER national survey of early childhood education services 2003–4. Wellington, NZ: NZCER.

Naldic.org.uk. (1999). [online] Available at: https://naldic.org.uk/wp-content /uploads/2020/01/NALDIC-Working-Paper-5-The-Distinctiveness-of -EAL_-a-cross-curriculum-discipline.pdf

NALDIC | EAL guidance | EYFS and EAL. (n.d.) https://www.naldic.org.uk/ eal-teaching-and-learning/outline-guidance/early-years/

Ng, Jennifer, Lee, Sharon, and Pak, Yoon. (2007). Chapter 4: Contesting the model minority and perpetual foreigner stereotypes: A critical review of literature on Asian Americans in education. *Review of Research in Education*, 31(1), 95–130.

Ochs, E. (1988). *Culture and Language Development: Language Acquisition and Language Socialization in a Samoan Village.* Cambridge: Cambridge University Press.

Ostrosky, M.M. and E.Y. Jung. (2005). Building positive teacher–child relationships. *What Works Briefs*. Center on the Social and Emotional Foundations for Early Learning. https://challengingbehavior.cbcs.usf.edu/ docs/whatworks/WhatWorksBrief_12.pdf

Palmer, J. (2014). Role play areas for early years foundation stage, key stage 1 and beyond. In Bower, V., *Developing Early Literacy 0–8.* London: Sage.

Piaget, J. (2007). (Originally published 1923) *The Language and Thought of the Child.* Translated by M. and R. Gabain. London: Routledge.

Powell, S. and Goouch, K. (2012). Whose hand rocks the cradle? Parallel discourses in the baby room. *Early Years*, 32(2), 113–127.

Promoting Young Children's Social and Emotional Health | NAEYC. https:// www.naeyc.org/resources/pubs/yc/mar2018/promoting-social-and -emotional-health

Quiroz, B. G., Snow, C. E., and Zhao, J. (2010). Vocabulary skills of Spanish-English bilinguals: Impact of mother-child language interactions and home language and literacy support. *International Journal of Bilingualism*, 14, 379–399.

Richtsmeier, P. T., Gerken, L. A., Goffman, L., and Hogan, T. (2009). Statistical frequency in perception affects children's lexical production. *Cognition*, 111, 372–377.

Roseberry, S., Hirsh-Pasek, K., and Golinkoff, R. M. (2013). Skype me! Socially contingent interactions help toddlers learn language. *Child Development*, 85, 956–970.

Saffran, J. R., Aslin, R. N., and Newport, E. L. (1996). Statistical learning by 8-month-old infants. *Science*, 274, 1926–1928.

Sethi, Raveewan. (2019). The Experiences of Third Culture Kids in Thailand. BSc Thesis. Assumption University of Thailand.

Shintani, N. (2012). Input-based tasks and the acquisition of vocabulary and grammar: A process-product study. *Language Teaching Research*, 16(2), 253–279.

Skinner, B. F. (1957). *Verbal Learning*. New York: Appleton-Century-Croft.

South, H. (2012). *NALDIC | EAL guidance | EAL specialist teachers and support staff*. [online] Naldic.org.uk. Available at: https://www.naldic.org.uk/eal-teaching-and-learning/outline-guidance/eal/

Stern, D., Spieker, S., and Mackain, C. (1982). Intonation contours as signals in maternal speech to prelinguistic infants. *Developmental Psychology*, 18: 727–735.

Swift, J. (1712). *A Proposal for Correcting, Improving and Ascertaining the English Tongue*. Menston, Yorkshire: Scolar Press.

Sylva, K., Melhuish, E., Sammons, P., Siraj Blatchford, I., and Taggart, B. (2004). *The Effective Provision of Pre-school Education (EPPE) Project: Findings from Preschool to End of Key Stage 1*. London: DfES/Institute of Education, University of London.

Tabors, P. O., Snow, C. E., and Dickinson, D. K. (2001). Homes and schools together: Supporting language and literacy development. In D. K. Dickinson and P. O. Tabors (eds), *Beginning Literacy with Language: Young Children Learning at Home and School* (pp. 313–334). Baltimore, MD: Paul H. Brookes Publishing.

Tabors, P. (1997). *One Child, Two Languages: A Guide for Preschool Educators of Children Learning English as a Second Language*. Baltimore, MD: Paul Brookes Publishing.

Tamis-LeMonda, C. S., Kuchirko, Y., and Song, L. (2014). Why is infant language learning facilitated by parental responsiveness? *Current Directions in Psychological Science*, 23, 121–126.

The Latino Family Literacy Project. (2021). Stephen Krashen's Monitor Model for Learning Language. [online] Available at: https://www.latinoliteracy .com/stephen-krashens-monitor-model-for-learning-language/

UKEssays. (2018). Chomsky's critical period for language acquisition. [online]. (November 2018). Available at: https://www.ukessays.com/ essays/english-language/critical-period-for-language-acquisition-english -language-essay.php?vref=1

Vygotsky, L. (1935). *Mind in Society: The Development of Higher Psychological Processes*. Cambridge, MA: Harvard University Press.

Weaver, G. R. (ed.) (2000). *Culture, Communication and Conflict: Readings in Intercultural Relations*, 2nd edition. Boston, MA: Pearson Publishing.

Weizman, Z. O. and Snow, C. E. (2001). Lexical input as related to children's vocabulary acquisition: Effects of sophisticated exposure and support for meaning. *Developmental Psychology*, 37, 265–279.

Wells, G. (1986). *The Meaning Makers: Children Learning Language and Using Language to Learn*. Sevenoaks, UK: Hodder and Stoughton.

Wells, G. (2009). *The Meaning Makers: Learning to Talk and Talking to Learn*. Bristol: Multilingual Matters.

Wintz, S. and Cooper, E. (2000–2003). *Learning Module Cultural and Spiritual Sensitivity: A Quick Guide to Cultures and Spiritual Traditions*. Available at: https://multifaiths.com/pdf/culturalsensitivity.pdf

4children. (2015). *What to Expect, When?*. 4children.org.uk. Available at: https://www.foundationyears.org.uk/files/2015/03/4Children_Parents Guide_2015_WEB.pdf

Index